SPOON CARVING

FROM LOG TO SPOON

Alex Finberg

SPOON CARVING

FROM LOG TO SPOON

THE CROWOOD PRESS

CONTENTS

INTRODUCTION

Carving spoons is a transformative journey for both the spoon-carver and for the wood itself. From the primal act of harvesting and splitting a log, to carving the wood into a refined spoon, a magical cycle is completed: from the life of a tree, to a freshly cut log, into a beautiful functional wooden spoon.

Taking a tree that was destined to rot or burn and transforming it into a wooden spoon engages the spoon carver in an interdependent relationship with the natural world, re-invigorating and re-establishing our connections to land, place and the web of life. This way of working 'green' wood offers an intimacy with the tree itself and its raw materials, which many of us hunger for.

In a world of neon screens and mass-produced items, carving spoons can help us find something ancient and profoundly humanising: *the opportunity to make beauty and meaning.*

Spoons themselves are inherently gentle and generous in their nature: cookers, stirrers, ladles, servers and eating spoons – all share traits designed to nourish. Many people have a favourite cooking spoon, or an heirloom eating spoon, passed down generations, which evokes a bond of fondness distinctly unique amongst everyday objects.

Spoon carving has become an extremely popular and increasingly accessible craft. The simplicity of working with a few basic hand tools at home or in the garden makes it compatible with busy modern lives. The internet has had a profound impact, accelerating the development of the craft. There is now a thriving international community of spoon carvers around the world. The new wood culture is bringing people together from diverse backgrounds, at spoon-carving festivals, workshops and local and online gatherings, uniting around the shared values of this truly sustainable and therapeutic craft.

There is no doubt about it – carving spoons is good for you.

This book is a manual on how to carve a wooden spoon from green wood. It provides a deep dive into the 25 steps I use to carve a log into a finished spoon, paying close attention to the skills and techniques needed to make beautiful wooden spoons.

WOOD

Trees are poems that the earth writes upon the sky.

– KAHLIL GIBRAN

The best wood for carving spoons is the wood that is both local and readily available. There is much to be learned from carving a variety of woods, as sharp tools and good technique can transform even seasoned firewood into beautiful spoons. However, when possible, it is recommended to choose green, recently felled wood. Carving green wood is not only easier on the hands and tools, but it also offers a primacy of connection to the tree itself and the unrivalled satisfaction of carving a freshly cut log into a finished spoon.

When selecting a tree species for spoon carving, the general rule is that hard woods make better spoons. It is advisable to avoid conifers in general, as their sap tends to gum up tools, and their fibrous nature makes them prone to unsatisfactory finishes. While hard woods are generally preferred, there are a few exceptions to this rule. Species such as Ash, Chestnut and Oak, despite being hard woods, do not lend themselves particularly well to spoon carving due to their ring-porous nature. These woods have small holes that can trap bacteria, making them less than ideal for cooking and eating spoons. That said, it can be fun to experiment and it is well worth carving a wide range of woods. There are some softer woods, such as Lime and Willow, which can provide a crisp and beautiful finish despite their softness and woods that will surprise and delight, such as Holly and Arbutus.

The satisfaction of trying to carve a new species is truly a journey of discovery: from the first split of the wood, you never quite truly know what you will unearth inside. The potential variations in colour, grain patterning and spalting can be remarkable.

My current favourites here in the UK are Beech, Holly, Mulberry and Cherry. These are followed closely by a long list of other wonderful species. Fruit woods, such as Plum, Apple, Pear, Apricot, Blackthorn and Hawthorn, tend to have beautiful heartwood and sapwood if you can find straight, knot-free pieces. So called 'plain' woods, such as Sycamore, Maple and London Plane, can be anything but plain, with shimmering rays and beautiful rippled grain patterns. Birch is a fantastic all-round wood, its bark making wonderful sheath material. It is one of the most reliable and versatile timbers to carve.

The table of wood species overleaf gives a list of tree species around the world that lend themselves well to spoon carving. This list has been compiled by spoon carvers in various locations around the world and is by no means exhaustive; it is well worth experimenting with whichever trees grow abundantly in your area.

Wood species for carving

Region	Tree Species	Latin Name	Pros	Cons
UK	Wild Cherry	*Prunus avium*	Beautiful heartwood	Sapwood can be plain
	Holly	*Ilex aquifolium*	Bakes beautifully	Greyish finish
	Hazel	*Corylus avellana*	Beautiful rays	
	Blackthorn	*Prunus spinosa*	Rainbow coloured heartwood	Small diameter, often twisted
	Sycamore	*Acer pseudoplatanus*	Beautiful shimmering rays	Dries and spalts very quickly
	Alder	*Alnus glutinosa*	Straight and easy to carve	Softish
	Willow (White)	*Salix alba*	Soft to carve	Soft
	Willow (Grey)	*Salix cinerea*	Soft to carve	Fibrous and tricky to finish
	Hawthorn	*Crataegus monogyna*	Beautiful creamy sapwood	Small diameter, often twisted
	Mulberry	*Morus nigra*	Lovely colours	Knotty and prone to inclusions
	Field Maple	*Acer campestre*	Stunning pale wood	Hard to carve
Europe	Beech	*Fagus sylvatica*	Carves beautifully	Spalting can turn soft
	Rowan	*Sorbus aucuparia*	Striking heartwood colours	Softer and prone to rot
	Lime	*Tilia x europaea*	Soft to carve	On the soft side
	Apple	*Malus x domestica*	Beautiful creamy sapwood	Prone to twists
	Pear	*Pyrus*	Lovely	Prone to twists
	Plum	*Prunus domestica*	Beautiful colours	Prone to twists & splitting
North America	Paper Birch	*Betula papyrifera*	Soft to carve yet finishes well	Dries out quickly
	Silver Maple	*Acer saccharinum*	Take a beautiful finish	Hard to carve dry
	Strawberry Tree	*Arbutus unedo*	Beautiful colours, slow growth	Prone to splitting
	Black Cherry	*Prunus serotina*	Beautiful heartwood colours	None
	Black Walnut	*Juglans nigra*	Beautiful dark heartwood	High silica content
	Lawson Cypress	*Chamaecyparis lawsoniana*	Lovely grain	Tiny knots & inclusions
South America	River Tamarind	*Leucaena leucocephala*	Beautiful grain & colours	Small diameter
	Peppertree	*Schinus molle*	Beautiful dark colours	An invasive species
	Guava	*Psidium guajava*	Lovely rich colours	Small diameter
	Bottlebrush Tree	*Callistemon*	Deep browns and creamy sapwood	Shrub sized tree
	Avocado	*Persea americana*	Gorgeous to carve, widespread	Hard
	Jurubeba	*Solanum paniculatum*	Pale and creamy wood	Prone to splitting
Middle East	Box Wood	*Buxus sempervirens*	Hard and carves beautifully	Hard to find large
	Olive Wood	*Olea europaea*	Hard and carves beautifully	Prone to splitting
	Willow Acacia	*Acacia salicina*	Soft to carve	On the softer side
	Neem Tree	*Azadirachta indica*	Beautiful reddish brown	Interlocking Grain

Region	Tree Species	Latin Name	Pros	Cons
	Loquat	*Eriobotrya japonica*	Stunning colours	Small diameter
	Christ's Thorn Jujube	*Ziziphus spina-christi*	Tight grained	Dense & prone to cracking
Caribbean	Seaside Mahoe	*Thespecia populnea*	Easy to carve, strong, and has some gorgeous colours	Hard to source
	Sapodilla	*Manilkara zapota*	Very strong, straight and tight grain, beautiful colour	Hard to source, very dense hard wood, tools require sharpening frequently when working
	Barbados Cherry	*Malpighia emarginata*	beautiful colour and finish	Difficult to get pieces big enough to work with
	Fiddlewood	*Citharexylum fruiticosum*	Consistent cream colour, strong	Can have a lot of knots to work around, tools require frequent sharpening
	Barbados Ebony	*Albezia lebbeck*	Beautiful colour, nice contrasting sapwood and heartwood, tree grows everywhere	Can sometimes be difficult to split larger pieces, tends to be a line of alternating grain direction between the sapwood and heartwood
	Seagrape	*Coccoloba unifera*	Carves easily, unique colour, common tree	Shrinkage is an issue, especially with smaller diameter pieces. Similar to guava wood but softer. Best to work with radially split billets
	Flamboyant	*Delonix regia*	Carves easily, unique yellow colour, common tree	On the lighter side, can be stringy, not as durable
Africa	Mango	*Magnifera indica*	easy to get hold of, Predictable to work with	grain can be quite twisted, making it difficult to split
	Guava	*PsidiumgGuajava*	Carves well, very strong, uniform colour	Very wet when freshly cut, needs time to dry out a bit, usually small diameter pieces
	Mahogany	*Swietenia mahogani*	easy to get hold of, predictable to work with	grain can be quite twisted, making it difficult to split
	Ebony	*Diospyros ebenum*	Beautiful colours	Very hard
Asia	Cypress	*Cupressus*	Beautiful grain	On the softer side
	Teak-Wood	*Tectona grandis*	Beautiful rich hues	Very hard
	Cedar	*Cedrus*	Aromatic beautiful grain	Prone to mini knots
	Rose-Wood	*Dalbergia nigra*	Beautiful colours	Prone to heartwood decay
	Sandal-Wood	*Santalum*	Fragrant and beautiful	On the softer side
Australasia	Banksia	*Proteaceae*	Spectacular grain patterns	Soft and pithy
	Camphor Laurel	*Cinnamomum camphora*	Rich honey-colour	Prone to grain tear out
	Magnolia	*Magnolia grandiflora*	Beautiful creamy colour	Soft and wide grain
	Silky Oak	*Grevillea robusta*	Stunning figuring	Blunts tools
	Queensland kauri	*Agathis robusta*	Clean and knotless	A protected timber
	Candlenut	*Aleurites moluccanus*	Soft and easy to work	Prone to rot

WOOD SELECTION

When searching for wood suitable for carving spoons, there are two main options to consider: bent branches, commonly known as crooks, or straight pieces of trunk. Crooks, with their naturally spoon-like shape, are particularly desirable. One of the key advantages of using crooks is that the grain of the wood often flows from the end of the handle through to the tip of the bowl in one graceful sweep. This unique characteristic not only enhances the beauty of the spoon but also contributes to its strength. Carving spoons from crooks captures the essence of Zen in the craft of spoon carving, combining both aesthetics and functionality in a harmonious manner.

Straight lengths of Cherry, freshly cut. These lengths are between 28cm and 30cm in diameter, sawn into 1m lengths and sealed and stored for future carving. They will be ideal for cooking spoons and eating spoons and feature throughout the book. Felled in autumn, they should remain optimal for carving for 9–14 months.

A ladle-sized crook. 15cm in diameter and 35cm in length, this will make a good small ladle or few smaller spoons with plenty of 'crank' in the handle. Searching for crooks from storm-fallen trees in the woods is a wonderful pastime!

A pile of recently felled green Cherry. The tree surgeons who felled the tree cut some of the branch and trunk wood into small 25cm sections; these will dry out fairly quickly and will need to be split and carved into eating spoons and scoops within three months for optimum carving.

It is possible to carve seasoned wood although it is harder on the hands and tools and not recommended for beginners. It is possible to re-soak wood though it won't be as soft as freshly cut 'green' wood. However, some woods are so special they are worth carving, even with minimal moisture content.

Bottom row (left to right): spalted Beech, Lime, Holly (baked), Cherry (sapwood), Strawberry Tree, Beech. Middle row (left to right): Oak, Ash, Arbutus Unedo, Blackthorn, Olive, Olive (baked). Top row (left to right): Hazel, Apple, Cherry.

GREEN WOOD

'Green wood working' established its roots way back in our ancestral past, arguably when the use of flint or stone hand tools became prevalent. Our ancestors had an intimate and reciprocal relationship with their natural resources, combined with a deep knowledge and 'primitive' skills set that ranged from cordage and basket-making to canoe building and round-wood timber framing. They knew instinctively to move on when an area of forest needed to regenerate, shaping the natural world as they went.

Spoon carving workshop in full swing.

Felling a tree by hand or with a flint axe requires patient diligence and one can safely assume that freshly felled wood, rather than seasoned timber, would have been the logical choice for many building and craft projects.

The enduring heritage of primitive and indigenous skills, centred around natural materials, serves as an inspiring example and holds great relevance in our present era as these skills embody the practice of genuine sustainability.

Today, the term 'green woodwork' refers to working with recently felled wood that retains a substantial level of sappy water content. This type of wood is well-suited to shaping and carving with hand tools. A visit to the hand tool museum in Troyes, France, reveals walls adorned with tools that are hundreds of years old; these tools have evolved in form and function over centuries, from ancient Egyptian draw-knives to seventeenth-century froes, but they are instantly recognisable to contemporary green woodworkers as the refined tools we use today.

Carving green wood offers a plethora of unexpected sensual delights. At this stage, the wood closely resembles a living limb, evident in its vitality, weight, texture and fragrance. Underneath the bark, the sticky wet sap reveals its freshness. The sound of fibres splitting as a log is cleft open with a mallet and froe can unveil a captivating array of colours within the sapwood and heartwood. Each wood species carries an unforgettable aroma, some more enticing than others: Cherry exudes a rich, marzipan scent; Hazel has a refreshing watermelon note; Chestnut hints at tomato sauce, whereas Tulip Poplar can smell like wet sheep's wool.

CRITERIA FOR SPOON CARVING WOOD

- Whole trees with branches intact are ideal.
- 1m lengths or longer with bark left on and ideally unscathed.
- 15cm in diameter or larger (rounds of wood larger than 35cm in diameter can be heavy and there can be more waste).
- Felled within the last three to six months (dependent on species and climate).
- Water content at 60 per cent or above.

A 25cm diameter Cherry log, sawn to 30cm in length, will be ideal for carving four to six cooking spoons. As this is fast-grown branch wood, with minimal heartwood, the spoons will be mainly sapwood.

A 30cm diameter Cherry log, with a large section of colourful heartwood. This should provide beautiful spoons in either tangential or radial planes.

This asymmetrical Cherry log, 30cm in diameter, should provide nine billets. Sketching out where to split the log will help maximise efficient splitting. This log should yield four radial billets and five tangential billets.

A larger 45cm diameter log of Cherry with rich heartwood colours. These logs are perhaps best for kuksas and bowls; however, it should provide a range of utensils from spatulas to large cooking spoons and ladles.

SOURCING WOOD

My phone book is filled with a diverse group of local tree surgeons who combine woodland management and domestic tree work, providing me with a consistent supply of excellent recently felled wood.

Living in urban areas, acquiring wood can be challenging, but trees are being felled every day, and they need to be utilised before they are turned into wood chips or firewood. Visiting the council depot, parks and gardens offices can be fruitful. It is worthwhile to establish connections with local arborists or orchard owners, approaching them with friendliness and clarity about your wood requirements.

When I lived in London, I used to send a group message to all the tree surgeons in my phone book. It would typically state: 'Hi, I'm a local green woodworker seeking 1m lengths of straight trunk or large limbs, measuring 14cm upwards in diameter. The wood should have been felled within the last three to six months. Most species, except for Ash, Oak and Chestnut, are great. I can pay cash on collection. Cheers!'

Most tree surgeons are willing to sell wood at the price of firewood; consider gifting them a spoon as well as cash to sow the seeds for a lasting relationship. While you're there, inquire about any landowners or coppice workers involved in woodland management, as well as local woodturners, landscapers, gardeners and orchard owners. These connections can be invaluable. Remember to keep your ears attuned to the sound of a chainsaw, and be prepared to drop everything in pursuit of freshly felled wood!

It is possible to buy wood and spoon blanks on the internet, but try to source wood from your own country and ideally from your own region. If sourcing green wood is challenging, it is possible to purchase seasoned Lime or Basswood blanks for spoon carving.

HARVESTING WOOD

Wherever you are in the world, and however great or small that perfectly spoon-shaped branch is, respecting the habitat and ecology of the woodland and acquiring the landowner's permission is essential before choosing to harvest any wood. I won't fell a tree simply because it would make some lovely spoons – local to me there are enough trees being cut each day for me to have a lifetime supply of wood without needing to fell or prune healthy living trees or buy exotic woods from the internet. Landowners are often felling trees and are all too happy to sell or give away a few bits of timber. After all, a single log, 40cm in length and 18cm in diameter will yield at least six large cooking spoons at minimum. I often keep a first aid kit, tarp, chainsaw, large saw, pocket saw, axe, work gloves and timber tongs in the boot just in case.

Bluebells growing in a Hazel coppice at the Wild Circle Retreat in Cornwall, UK – home to a diverse array of plants and wildlife and a sustainable source of quality timber for building, firewood and craft production.

Storing wood

The best time of year for harvesting and storing wood is late-autumn, at this point the trees are beginning to rest for winter and their water and sap content is no longer rising. You'll then have the whole winter and spring ahead to work through your stash. A tree which has come down in late spring or summer is full of sappy water, it is best left to 'mellow' and rest for a month or two. The process of mellowing is akin to the ripening of fruit: the wood softens a little as the grain fibres relax and the sapwood colours tend to deepen to richer hues. Mellow cherry makes for wonderful carving and the window with which to work it is pretty long: three months to two years or even more. However, species prone to rotting, such as Beech, require splitting and carving before the spalting process turns the wood 'punky' and brittle.

Sealing the end grain of logs with non-toxic PVA glue helps seal in moisture content and prevent the wood from drying out.

Once a tree is cut down and processed into timber, it begins to dry out immediately. The rate at which it does so is dependent on a range of factors, including tree species, season, local climate and the lengths at which it is cut (try to stop tree surgeons slabbing up timber into 30cm lengths – they mean well, assuming it will be used for firewood, but the longer the lengths the better for us green wood workers!).

As a general rule when sourcing wood, the greener the better. The question is how to slow the process of drying sufficiently to keep your supply 'green', whilst preventing checking and cracking. The good news is wood retains water content fairly well when left 'in the round', in long lengths, stored in a cool damp place, off the ground and out of direct sunlight and covered with a tarp or in a wood shed. The sides should be left open for air to circulate to prevent fungi moving in.

The end of your logs (the end grain) can be sealed with beeswax, leftover paints or nontoxic PVA glue. This will help slow the drying and prevent checking and cracking.

Drying and shrinkage

It is common to work with green wood, which has a moisture content of between 30 and 60 per cent. You can find out by using a digital moisture meter, or by simply picking up the log: if it is full of water it will feel heavy. Scrape the bark of and see how much moisture is under the bark, and saw and split a small section 10cm from the end of the log to see how much moisture is in the core and how deep the checks (cracks in the end grain) run. Good firewood has less than 20 per cent moisture content, anything under 20 per cent will be tough carving but is nonetheless doable, just keep your tools sharp and use efficient technique – certain special pieces are worth going the extra mile for!

It can be easy to become hung up on the percentages of moisture content, but if the wood is in log form – preferably in longer lengths – and has been felled in the last three to six months, in a mild or cool climate, it should prove reliably 'green'. In hotter, drier climates it may be necessary to split the wood into billets and store in a freezer, or use within a shorter time frame.

End grain checking and cracking. This log has been drying outdoors uncovered for over 18 months. Its moisture content will be roughly 25–35 per cent and the cracks and checking will probably extend into the log. The log should be topped and tailed, and care will need to be taken to avoid the existing cracks.

Soaking spoon blanks in a bucket of water for 48 hours helps soften the wood a little and increase carve-ability.

When green wood dries, hygroscopic shrinkage takes place. This means that wood, almost like a sponge, will gain or lose moisture dependent upon the variable humidity, temperatures and conditions of the surrounding air and environment. The species of tree, whether the logs are in the round, how long the lengths of wood are, how shady your storage shed is, and how much PVA glue you've used to seal its end grain, are all key factors.

The other aspect of wood's hygroscopicity is that it dries in a non-uniform way. First it loses its 'free water' contained in the pores of the wood, which hardly causes any shrinkage at all. The log will be dry on the outside, and wet on the inside (this is called a moisture gradient). From this point the wood starts to lose its 'bound water', which is trapped within the cell walls. The dry outer sapwood and bark wants to shrink as it dries below the fibre saturation point; however, the wetter heartwood or 'core' constrains it, causing 'checks' to form on the end grain. Once the heartwood core wants to shrink, the outer rings constrain it and check form at the core also.

Once a piece of wood is split, it will dry differently in its varying planes. Along its longitudinal plane, or lengthwise down the billet, shrinkage is negligible, between 0.1 and 0.3 per cent. However radial shrinkage can range from 3 to 6 per cent and tangential shrinkage from 6 to 12 per cent. This can be evident in the 'cupping', which can occur in spoon bowls as they dry. The best way to mitigate this is to leave plenty of material on the underside of the spoon bowl as it dries. Any asymmetry created from cupping can then be evened out once the spoon has stabilised.

Soaking wood

It can be frustrating when your wood supply dries out beyond the point of being mellowed into seasoned firewood. However, there is good news: soaking billets is a viable solution. There are various methods to reintroduce moisture into wood. One option is to create a 50/50 mix of water and alcohol, but a simpler, cheaper approach of soaking the billets or spoon blanks in a bucket of water for two to three days will suffice. To ensure thorough saturation, use a brick or a heavy weight to keep them fully submerged.

Carving soaked wood presents a slightly different experience compared to working with mellowed wood. Re-soaked billets possess a subtle brittleness. However, the process is certainly worthwhile as it is highly rewarding to salvage your spoon blanks from the confines of the log pile and enjoy a softer, more forgiving carve. Some caution is required when letting re-soaked billets dry as they can crack; this can be mitigated by placing them in a plastic bag or container.

'Reading the grain' in a piece of radially split Cherry. Focusing primarily on the longitudinal cells it is easy to see where a knot was present in the bottom right corner. This section will be discarded.

GRAIN DIRECTION

In simple terms, 'grain' refers to the arrangement of wood fibres within a tree. Imagine a cartoon image of a perfectly straight tree, where the wood fibres run vertically from the base of the trunk to the top. As the tree's limbs reach out in a spiral motion to seek optimal light, the grain becomes wiggly and irregular.

As the tree grows, the cambium acts as a wood factory, producing two types of wood cells: longitudinal cells and ray cells. Longitudinal cells, as the name suggests, are long and function as thin tubes, carrying sap vertically up and down the tree, from the roots to the leaves. In contrast, ray cells run in parallel across the tree and serve as hollow pathways, transporting sap and minerals across the heartwood and sapwood. They also support tyloses, which are the tree's response to injury and provide resistance to decay.

Different tree species grow in distinct ways based on their environment. As a result, the direction and orientation of their wood cells, or grain, can vary significantly. Visualise a European woodland with tall, straight beech trees competing for light in the canopy, contrasting with the twisted and gnarled form of a plum tree in a spacious orchard, or the spiralling shape of a eucalyptus tree.

Radial vs tangential cleaving

It is crucial to learn how to identify the grain direction in a piece of wood and how to carve in relation to that direction. Depending on how a log is split or cleft, the presentation of the grain direction will vary between different planes in the wood. Fortunately, once a log is split, the concept of grain quickly becomes intuitive to grasp.

We will explore in detail how to split and carve a log into a wooden spoon in Chapters 4 and 5. It is important first to explore the concept of growth rings and how grain direction orientates in two key planes in a log.

Planning how a log is going to be split minimises waste and maximises the potential for beautiful spoons. 'T' for tangential blanks and 'R' for radial blanks.

Left: a radially split 'flat' billet. Right: a tangentially split 'wedge shaped' billet.

A radially split billet and spoon carved in the radial plane. The grain lines run straight through the bowl and handle.

The radial plane

The radial plane contains grain that is perpendicular to the growth rings. The radial plane is easy to remember as the grain can be visualised as 'radiating' out from the centre of the pith to the bark. A piece of radially split wood will have what is called long (hopefully) straight grain running down its length. A spoon carved from a radially split billet will have the growth rings running vertically through the handle and bowl.

Pros

Larger diameter wood (30cm and over) with straight grain running through it, such as Maple, Beech and Poplar, can produce large amounts of clean and reliable radial billets – ideal for making lots of identical spoons for production carving.

Radially carved spoons can show off tonal contrast between the sapwood and the heartwood; having the darker heartwood on one side of the bowl and the creamy white sapwood on the other can be very pretty.

Cons

With grain running through the length of the spoon, radially carved spoons might appear strong. However, if we were to zoom in on the leading edge of the spoon bowl, we would see a line of open-ended grain fibres. These can be visualised as severed drinking straws; over time they can become damaged and even crack from repeated scraping the bottoms of cooking pots and pans. This can be compensated for to an extent by leaving a thick chamfered edge on the spoon that will stand up to rigorous scraping and scrambling.

The other areas of weakness in a radially carved spoon are the edges of the bowl, which are liable to cracking at the very edge of the handle.

The tangential plane

The tangential plane contains grain that is parallel to the growth rings. A tangentially cleft piece of wood is typically wedge shaped, and a spoon is carved from a tangential billet 'bark up'. If a spoon is carved in a tangential piece upside down with the bark at the back of the bowl, this is known as a reverse tangentially carved spoon. A tangentially cleft piece will present entirely different growth rings to a radially split spoon; they are circular or oval in shape and can be beautiful. A spoon carved from a tangentially split billet will have circular growth rings in the bowl itself.

A tangentially split billet and spoon carved in the tangential plane. The concentric rings show up beautifully in the bowl.

Pros

The sight of growth rings in the bowl of tangentially carved spoons, orientated with the heartwood in the centre of the bowl is aesthetically pleasing, particularly when there is a rich variation in hues and colour tones. Tangential spoons can be more resilient in their bowls, a key factor in cooking spoons.

Cons

Tangentially carved spoons also have weak spots. This is particularly true the more 'crank' or curve is in the spoon. This is because the spoon will likely have to cut across the grain, making the spoon inherently weaker than a spoon carved from a bent branch, where the grain runs from the top of the handle through to the tip of the bowl. A spoon with these weak spots can be described as having 'short grain'. The neck of a cooking spoon is particularly vulnerable to snapping if it has been carved with short grain and no compensation has been made in the design of the spoon (such as accentuating the depth of the keel).

PRINCIPLES OF WORKING WITH WOOD GRAIN

Once grasped, the principles of grain direction are transferable across the entire spectrum of woodworking, from round-wood timber framing to dovetail joinery and furniture making.

Identify the grain direction

Understanding the grain direction is essential for making informed design decisions. Before you start carving, carefully observe the wood and determine the direction in which the grain runs. This can be done by examining the tree as it grows or the log as it is split, or by looking at the billet in front of you.

Going with the grain

Carving with the grain, or parallel to the wood fibres, is generally easier. It reduces the risk of tear-out and your tools will slice through the wood more smoothly. A general principle to adhere to is you can't carve smoothly 'uphill' – this will cause your tool to get stuck or 'tear out' the wood, where the wood fibres break or splinter. Just before this happens, simply turn the spoon around and come back in the opposite direction.

Cross-grain cuts

Carving across the grain, or perpendicular to the wood fibres, requires more effort and sharp tools (as ever) are essential. Carving across the grain increases the chances of tear-out. It is my preferred method for hollowing out spoon bowls.

Splitting a Cherry log with a froe: the split is following a twist in the grain.

A radially split billet with a slight twist in the grain.

Grain orientation affects strength

The orientation of the grain can impact the strength and stability of your spoon. As mentioned earlier, we have the choice to carve either from a radial or tangential piece of wood – but we also have the choice of where to orientate the spoon within the piece of wood. We will cover this in further detail in Chapter 4.

Grain affects appearance

Consider how the grain interacts with the overall design and use it to your advantage to create visually pleasing effects, such as the rings in the bowl of a tangentially carved spoon.

A pile of radial and tangential cherry billets.

A wedge-shaped tangential billet.

Grain irregularities and knots

Be aware of any grain irregularities, such as knots or interlocking fibres, as they can pose challenges during carving. Knots are usually denser and harder than the surrounding wood, and the grain direction will often deviate to accommodate them. This requires special attention to avoid mishaps.

Grain orientation (side profile)

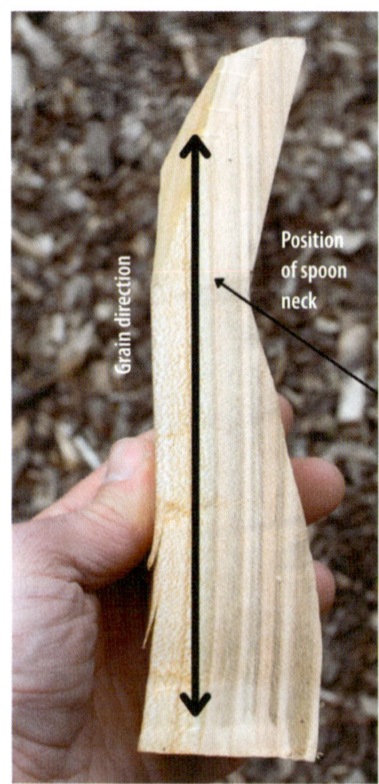

The grain running along the side of a spoon billet.

Tricky grain

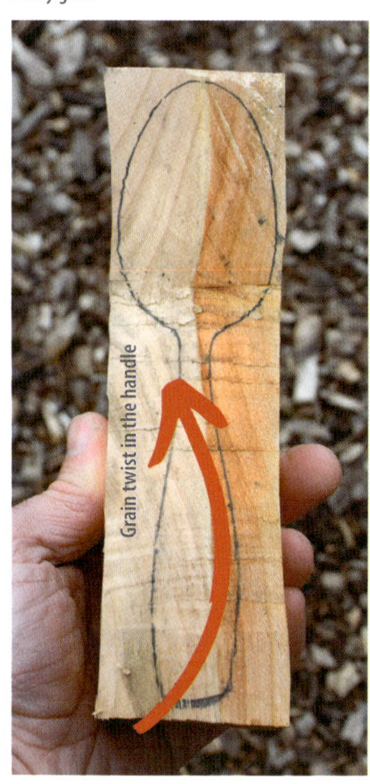

Grain can twist and 'run out' from the spoon, causing difficulty carving.

Carving with the grain

A radially carved eating spoon.

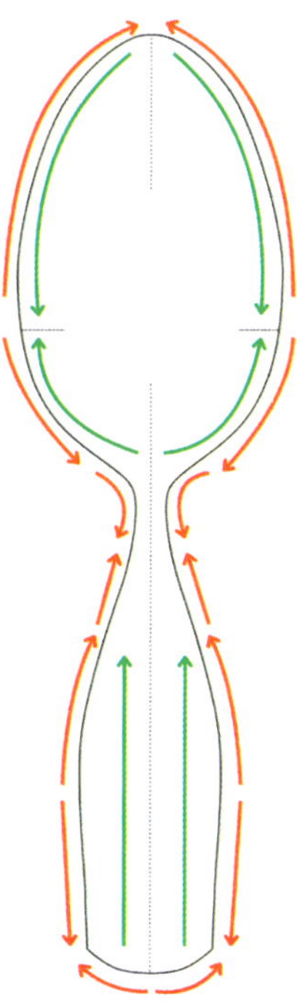

Red: carving the side profile of the spoon. Green: carving the top profile.

SPALTING

'Spalting' refers to the unique and visually striking patterns that occur in certain types of decaying wood, typically caused by fungal activity. During the early stages of decomposition, fungi colonise the wood, breaking down its cell structure and releasing enzymes that interact with the wood's pigments. This interaction results in a range of captivating colours and intricate patterns, including dark 'zone' lines, streaks, and areas of contrasting hues. Spalting can create visually stunning effects, transforming ordinary wood with strikingly unique patterns. However, while spalting enhances the aesthetic appeal of wood, it can also compromise its structural integrity if left unchecked. The point of no return is when the wood becomes soft and 'punky' and it is too far gone to be effective for spoon carving.

Left: spalted Beech billets. Right: the end grain of a spalted Beech log.

An array of cook-and-serve and asymmetric cooking spoons, carved with axe and knife from spalted Beech wood.

Close-up of spalted Beech spoons with unique patterns created by fantastic fungi.

RECLAIMED WOOD

Carving reclaimed wood can be rewarding, but fraught with risks; it is also harder going on the hands and tools. I would not recommend carving reclaimed wood as a beginner. You might well be put off by how hard the wood is, and being able to maintain a sharp edge on your tools is crucial as they will dull more quickly.

When selecting reclaimed wood, it is crucial to identify if any nails, screws or other debris are buried in the wood: they may not be visible, and it would be far from ideal chipping the edge of your axe on one. Clean the timber of dust and debris by soaking and rinsing it, saw down your billet to an appropriate size, and carve the spoon blank with a hatchet.

The joy of reclaimed timber is that you may be able to work with exotic woods. I have enjoyed carving Ebony, Mahogany, Iroko and Rimu – all woods that have a unique character of their own and do not grow abundantly (if at all) in the UK.

Oak spoon carved from 150-year-old floor joists from a Cornish dwelling. The Oak itself could have been growing 400–800 years ago, or more.

TROUBLESHOOTING AND FAQS

How long will wood stay green and fresh?

This is dependent on the humidity and air temperature, level of shade, how dry the wood is kept and how long the lengths are, and it is hard to give a concrete answer. I collect 1m lengths of freshly felled Beech and Cherry in the autumn. The Cherry can be stored for a year or so like this, and although it will lose a lot of moisture in this time, will be possible to carve. The Beech will start to spalt in six months or so. Sycamore dries out pretty quickly and is best carved fresh. Certain species, such as Lime and Willow, carve well even when seasoned.

Why is my wood going mouldy?

Spalting is coloration caused by the presence of mycorrhizal fungi in the wood. Spalting can be immensely pretty or quite ugly depending on your taste and the species. Sycamore tends to develop blue speckled spots quite quickly, whereas spalted Beech is famously beautiful for the black 'zone lines' competing fungi lay down, which create unique and striking patterns in the wood. It is possible to speed up the process of spalting by placing rounds of Beech in bin bags. Split a test piece every now and then; there is such a thing as too much spalting, as it can make the wood weaker and unsuitable for spoons.

Can I eat from spalted wood?

Once the spoon has dried out, the fungus is dormant in the wood. Although the fungi aren't dead, they are no longer reproducing spores and any current spores in the spoon wood will be sealed in by your chosen oil. There is absolutely nothing wrong with using spalted wood for food items – as long as it is properly dried and sealed, it is non-toxic and food safe.

How do I best prevent my wood from cracking?

Various organic wood sealants and non-toxic PVA glue options are available. Apply your chosen sealant to the ends of your logs with a paintbrush, keep your wood in a covered dry area, out of direct sunlight and wind, and you have done the best you can to slow the inevitable.

Can I freeze my wood?

Splitting your logs into billets (see Chapter 4) and then freezing them is a viable option. Once out of the freezer, carve them immediately and be sure to dry your spoon blanks slowly in wood chip or a plastic bag.

Can I buy spoon blanks?

Many carvers today offer green, axed-out spoon blanks, which can be purchased online or in person. Try to buy locally and if possible, find a spoon carving workshop near you and learn to axe the billets out yourself – the satisfaction of axe carving is not to be missed!

TOOLS

Use the right tool, for the right job, in the right way.

– PROVERB

From the first split of a log with a froe, to the last finishing cut with a knife, the entire process of carving a spoon is principally an exercise in splitting and slicing, until you have removed all the wood that isn't a spoon. The cleaner the split of the fibres, the better the finished spoon. Sharp tools, good technique and practice are key to carving beautiful spoons.

The refreshing thing about spoon carving is that with four simple tools and an axe block and mallet you can make beautiful functional spoons in your living room or back yard, without the need for loud, dusty power tools or a workshop filled with expensive tools. This makes spoon carving affordable and accessible.

This chapter offers a comprehensive description of tools that offer versatile options for spoon carvers on a range of budgets and abilities. The bottom line is that skill and sharp tools will go further than simply having the highest quality tools. There are a number of options for spoon carvers on a budget, particularly if you are willing to put in the time to learn how to re-grind and sharpen vintage tools or mass-produced tools that have been verified to be worth re-purposing.

There are a great many tools that claim to be made for spoon carving but unfortunately have been designed badly, or are produced to substandard condition with low quality steel; these are therefore inappropriate and sometimes dangerous.

The tools I recommend in this book I can stand behind as tried, tested and recommended. Ultimately you get what you pay for, and budget tools will have their limitations. We are fortunate to be in the midst of a resurgence in tool making with talented tool makers making an array of quality tools specifically for green wood working and spoon carving. So as soon as the spoon carving bug catches, be sure to support tool makers in their craft and invest in high quality tools.

Carving a spoon blank on a simple three-legged chopping block. The simplest design is a hardwood top, with three mortise holes drilled in at an angle and three 8cm-diameter legs with tapered tenons, which can be removed for ease of transportation.

Carving on a full-sized bowl mule, built on similar principle to a three-legged block, but with four legs, and holes drilled for pegs that hold bowls and kuksas, much like a modern workbench with wooden wedges for clamps.

AXE BLOCKS

It is very easy to overlook making an adequate axe block in the excitement of making your first spoons. I know people who have been carving for years on a block with wonky legs, at the wrong height, which is a bit like riding a donkey when you could ride a horse: it'll get you there, but you'll have a smoother, swifter ride and your body will thank you for a proper chopping block.

You can work sitting down or standing at a block. I recommend the latter unless you struggle to stand for periods of time. Standing will give you better posture and enable you to use the mechanics of your body efficiently. The block should be made from a hardwood, such as Ash or Oak. Perhaps the simplest approach is to use one large tree stump cut flush at both ends; however, they are very hard to manoeuvre alone and not as stable as a tripod block with legs.

How to make an axe block

To ascertain the correct the height of your axe block, extend your arm by your side and clench your fist: the height of your block should be the distance between the ground and your knuckles. This height can be surprisingly low, but it supports the most efficient swing of your axe.

Note this measurement, and work out the length of your legs, plus the height of your chopping block, minus 6cm for the leg mortises.

Keep your block clean!

Keep your carving block clean and free of debris. Timber picks up all kinds of grit and debris from the moment it is felled. I have found tiny stones, grit from soil, barbed wire, air rifle pellets and old fencing when splitting wood and my axe never thanked me for it. Take care of your shaving sharp axe by keeping it for carving billets only; use an old hatchet for splitting and bark removal.

Select a hardwood log, such as Ash or Oak, a minimum of 30cm in diameter and 35cm in height. For solidity a larger log can be used but the compromise will be in the manoeuvrability of a large heavy log. Well-seasoned timber is preferable as it is less likely to crack and check than greener wood.

Select three round-wood legs 10cm in diameter, straight and free of knots. Chestnut makes very durable leg material. Cut to length using the height measuring equation above. Mark the ends of the legs with a 25mm circle with a compass for a tapered tenon (or 1in if using a 1in tenon cutter).

Mark three holes. Pilot drill a 20 degree angle with a drill bit. Using a bevel gauge helps guide you to drill the correct angle. The angle of your legs depends on the height vs stability ratio and should range from between 20–35 degrees. Drill the mortises (holes) with a 25mm or 1in drill bit for a 1in tenon, T Auger, or spade bit, 100mm deep.

Using a shave-horse and draw-knife, shape the legs into tapered tenons, or use a tenon cutter. This can also be done with an axe. Carve the legs into octagonal facets on your axe block. Then finish with a knife.

Mark up a triangle on the block. Mark three holes. Pilot drill a 20-degree angle with a drill bit. Using a bevel gauge helps guide you to drill the correct angle. The angle of your legs depends on the height vs stability ratio and should range from 20 to 35 degrees. Drill the mortises (holes) 10cm deep with a 25mm (or 1in) drill bit, T auger, or spade bit.

Tap the legs into the mortises. Stand the block up on flat ground and saw down your legs to the appropriate height with a plank for a guide.

SHAVE HORSES, SPOON MULES AND VICES

A 'dumb-head' shave-horse is a versatile shave horse used for a range of green wood working tasks and enables the use of a draw-knife or spokeshave. Top left: the limitations of this design mean only three quarters of the spoon can be worked at one time, unlike a dedicated spoon mule.

These shave horse designs are really only suitable for longer cooking spoons, but offer a wonderfully efficient alternative to the rigours of axe and knife carving.

A folding shave horse built by Peter Lanyon based on the Origami Shave Horse by Green Wood Lab (Gifu, Japan).

As the name suggests, these shave horses fold away neatly and can be hung on the wall or stored under the bed!

Spoon mule: an adaption of the shave horse, a spoon mule is specifically designed for spoon carvers wishing to use drawknives, push knives, twca cams and spokeshaves to carve spoons. Spoon mule built by Dominic Pearce (Cornish woodsmith) based on plans by Dawson Moore (Michigan Sloyd).

Spoon mules use a foot-enabled vice to clamp the spoon firmly in place with jaws which allow for draw-knives, spokeshaves and push knives to be used for efficient carving along the entire length of the spoon without restriction.

Spoon mules can be particularly effective in carving large volumes of cooking spoons and spatulas with straight handles.

Having a sturdy clamp allows for efficient stock removal and the shaping of convex shapes like the back of this cook and serve spoon.

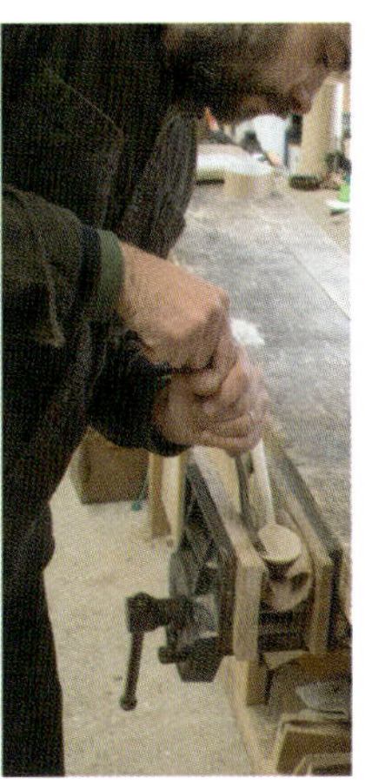

Left: a workbench and vice can provide an ideal setup for carving with curved gouges.
Right: a close-up of a coffee scoop being carved with a Kirschen Tools curved gouge.

Stock knife by Sean Hellman. A stock knife uses mechanical leverage to slice, much like a clog-maker's *paroir* or stock knife. This knife has a shorter blade which has been hollow ground on the back bevel for ease of sharpening.

Sjöbergs Smart Workstation Pro: a versatile portable workbench is a good option when space is tight. It can be moved and clamped down to any surface and comes complete with a wide vice, bench dogs and ample work surface. It's ideal for compact spaces and on-site projects for those without a full workbench setup.

A curved gouge is used to carve the bowl from a leaf-shaped cooking spoon. Having a smart vice can be particularly helpful for carving harder woods and relieving strain from carving with hook tools.

Bow saws

Bow saws with a blade length of between 50–80cm are great all-round saws for cutting billets to size. The larger sized saws can be used in tandem, and two people can make light work of relatively wide diameter logs.

Crosscut saws

The satisfaction of sawing your own timber with a crosscut saw is phenomenal. Ditch the chainsaw, and employ your friend or partner to join you in good exercise, team building and the wholesome pursuit of timber processing.

Top to bottom: Japanese Hassunme 265mm pull saw; Samurai Saws Ichigeki C-330 pruning saw; Tajima G-Saw™ 210mm folding saw; Silky Pocketboy 170 folding pocket saw. Japanese saws cut on the pull stroke, in contrast to conventional Western saws. The bottom image shows how the teeth are orientated towards the handle, enabling an accurate and efficient pull cut.

Pull saws

Pull saws are also used in China, Turkey and other countries, but the Japanese *nokogiri* have been refined over centuries for precise sawing for joinery. The advantage of pull saws is their accuracy and the ability to leave a narrower cut (or kerf) in the timber. Pull saw blades differ: *yokobiki* is a cross-cutting blade designed to cut across the grain of the wood; *tatebiki* blades are designed for 'ripping' down the grain of the wood.

Folding saws range from the Silky Pocketboy with a 17cm blade for sawing billets, up to the Silky Bigboy with a 36cm blade capable of sawing through rounds of larger timber.

For the longest time I have foregone a chainsaw and have got by with a 32-inch bow saw, a 210mm folding saw and a Japanese crosscut pull saw. These took care of all my sawing needs.

Chainsaws

Although chainsaws are not a necessary piece of kit for the spoon carver, they are ruthlessly efficient at felling trees and sawing logs to length. If you are going to delve into other aspects of green wood work or use firewood, they are a worthwhile investment. To cover the vast array of different saws is beyond the scope of this book, but as with all tools, having the right tool for the right job is essential. Chainsaws should be carefully selected along the following guidelines:

- I do not recommend buying a second-hand saw, if you are a first-time buyer. Unfortunately, chainsaws can be neglected or have hidden damage, which can prove costly or dangerous.
- I would strongly recommend taking a chainsaw maintenance and cross cut course at minimum, or appropriate to the diameter of trees you are intending to fell.
- Buy all of the adequate PPE, and always use it, with no exceptions. Even small battery saws can have chain-speeds up to 17m/s. Just because it's electric doesn't mean it can't give severe or life-threatening injuries.
- Service the saw every season or after heavy use and maintain a sharp chain at all times.

Two ends of the chainsaw spectrum. Top: Dewalt Electric, 18V XR Brushless Chainsaw with 30cm bar which runs off 5Ah batteries for occasional, domestic use sawing logs up to 30cm. Bottom: Stihl 660 Professional Petrol Saw, for professional sawing of large diameter timber.

Essential chainsaw personal protection (PPE) includes: a safety helmet with eye and ear protection; chainsaw gloves; chainsaw trousers or chaps for leg and groin protection; chainsaw boots.

Chainsaw sharpening and maintenance tools. Left to right: Oregon Tools chain measuring guide; Oregon magnetic 30-degree guide; a fencing tack for measuring pitch.

TOOLS FOR SPLITTING WOOD

Froe

Froes are used in combination with a wooden mallet in a range of cleaving applications, from splitting small diameter lengths of Hazel for hurdle making to splitting large rounds of chestnut for making roof shingles. They are wonderfully safe and accurate for splitting spoon blanks. A long handle can really support the lever action required to cleave open larger diameter logs.

Splitting wedges

Splitting wedges are invaluable for cleaving green wood. Metal wedges should not be struck with a metal sledge hammer as the polls or back of the wedges will be rounded over, and soon become susceptible for sending metal shrapnel flying went struck. This is to be avoided; instead, strike with a wooden maul! Wooden wedges can be used with a sledge hammer but are disposable and prone to cracking.

Hatchet

Using a hatchet for splitting can save the edge of your carving axe, and is particularly handy for bark removal and cutting recalcitrant fibres in a half-split log, and can be a stand-in for splitting wedges.

Mallet

A wooden mallet, also known as a beetle, maul or bodger's basher, is used in combination with an axe, splitting wedge or froe to split wood. A wooden mallet has the advantage of not damaging the steel of the tools. There is little more cringe-inducing than hearing a sledge hammer smashing against the back of a froe! This causes the steel of the froe to mushroom over, damaging the spine of the froe and limiting the longevity of the tool.

How to make a mallet

Wooden mallets can be made quickly from gnarly grained fruit wood, Oak, or Holly or hardwood roots: the gnarlier the grain the longer the mallet will last. I made the mistake of making a mallet from a lovely piece of straight-grained Beech, it lasted about 2 months, whereas a hefty mallet with gnarly grain should last for years.

It is also possible to simply drill a 30mm hole through a large lump of gnarly wood and fit a long straight handle with a wedge, much like a sledgehammer. These longer-handled mauls can be useful for cleaving large logs in combination with metal or wooden splitting wedges.

Tools for splitting. Left to right: 'Ray Iles' froe; metal splitting wedges; wooden splitting wedges; small mallet (Ash); 1¾lb restored 'Elwell' hatchet; large mallet (Holly). Coated with red linseed oil paint for visibility.

Select a piece of seasoned knotty wood, such as such as Apple, Plum, Holly or hardwood root, 15cm in diameter and cut to 60cm in length.

Remove the bark with an axe or with a draw knife and saw in a stop cut approximately 2cm deep around the entire diameter.

Shape the handle of the mallet by carving down from the stop cut to the end of the handle in long facets. Start by carving an octagonal handle. It helps to draw your desired handle diameter on the bottom of the handle to act as a guide.

Turn the mallet around and shape the handle by carving down to the saw cut, continuing to make octagonal facets. Take care not to over-strike into the head of the mallet.

Carve the corners of the facets with a knife and make a round handle that feels comfortable in the hand.

Sealing the end of the mallet with non-toxic PVA glue or linseed oil paint will help prevent cracking and make the mallet visible in large piles of woodchip!

ESSENTIAL TOOLS FOR SPOON CARVING

Two shoestring budget kits. Kit 1: (from left to right): Irwin Saw, Mora 120 Knife, Mora 164 Single Bladed Hook Knife, Bahco Axe. Kit 2: (from left to right): Samurai Saw, Mora 120 Knife, Mora 164 Single Bladed Hook Knife, Prandi Axe. Both Axes are sold blunt and require extensive grinding and sharpening to carve with.

Make-your-own kit. From left to right: Tajima G-Saw 210mm folding pull saw; Nic Westermann sloyd blade (hand-carved Cherry handle); Wood Tools open curve hook knife blade (handled with Wild Cherry); Eagle Edge Tool Co. vintage 1lb Kent pattern axe (with 30cm Ash haft). Budget-friendly and top quality, requires tool handling skills.

Recommended off-the-shelf kit. Left to right: Silky Pocketboy folding pull saw; Wood Tools Robin Wood compound curve hook knife; Mora 106 knife; and Wood Tools Robin Wood carving axe. Fantastic value-for-money kit with good quality tools.

The author's core carving tools: Hans Karlsson axe, Svante Djärv adze, Nic Westermann open curve hook knife, Hans Karlsson hook knife, Nic Westermann Sloyd knife.

The author's carving tools: Hans Karlsson axe, Svante Djarv adze, 45mm adze, Oscar Rush 50mm adze, Hans Karlsson hook knife and sloyd knife, Tajima folding saw, Nic Westermann sloyd knife, Hewn and Hone finishing knife and turning sloyd, Nic Westermann open curve hook knife and roughing hook.

CARVING AXES

One of the most satisfying aspects of spoon carving is the use of a carving axe. Due to the developments of modern machinery in carpentry and building, the application and uses of axes has declined in modern times. However, an axe is a tool capable of felling a tree and building a home, and axes still perform important roles in modern woodland management: felling, splitting, snedding, pleaching, in bushcraft, axe throwing and timber sports, in Viking re-enactments and so on!

Carving axes are made entirely differently from the axes used in splitting timber for firewood. Even everyday hatchets aren't suitable for carving spoons. This is due to a number of factors, primarily the bevel edged 'profile' and geometry (which we'll cover in detail in Chapter 3), the quality of steel used, the length of the handle and the weight of the axe head. It is possible to modify some hatchets into carving axes, which I'll demonstrate later on in this chapter, but there isn't really a substitute for a dedicated carving axe.

Soulwood Creations carving axe #2.

Recommended carving axes

Maker	Axe	Country	Bevel	Cutting Edge	Weight	Handle	Wood	Sheath
Gränsfors Bruk	Large carving axe	Sweden	Convex bevel	110mm	1kg	355mm	American Hickory	Leather, popper
Hans Karlsson	Slöjd axe	Sweden	Flat over hollow, 30 degrees	100mm	700g	370mm	Elm	Leather
Svante Djärv	Little Viking axe	Sweden	Flat: 27–28 degrees	140mm	800g	330mm	Swedish Elm/Ash	Leather, popper
Julia Kalthoff	Small carver	Sweden	Flat: 30–32 degrees slight concave	130mm	550g	300mm	Swedish Ash	Veg tanned Bordeaux leather
James Wood	Socketed carver	UK	Flat	130mm	900g	400mm	Hickory	Veg tanned leather
Josh Burrell	Light carving axe	UK	Flat	114mm	600g	300mm	English Ash	
Oscar Rush	Small carving axe	UK	Flat	95–100mm	600g	280mm	English Ash	
Wood Tools	Robin Wood carving axe	UK	Slight convex	110mm	720g	310mm	Hickory	Leather, popper
Wood Tools	Large carving axe	UK	Slight convex	110mm	975g	350mm	Hickory	Leather, popper
Soulwood Creations	Carving axe	UK	Flat 30 degrees	140mm	750g	310mm	Ash	Leather, popper
Strong Way Tools	Carving axe	Ukraine	Flat 30 degrees	150mm	1007g	380mm	Ash	Leather, stud

It is a wonderfully exhilarating experience using a dedicated razor-sharp axe to carve wood and a there is a range of carving axes forged and ground especially for green wood and spoon carving. Identifying the right choice of axe involves weighing up a combination of your budget, strength, accuracy and personal taste.

Key differentiating factors of carving axes involve the following:

- The maker
- The steel used
- Forging and heat treatment
- Bevel grind
- Dimensions of the head: edge profile, length of cutting edge
- Head weight
- Handle: dimensions, wood choice and grain orientation
- Sheath

Left: Gränsfors Bruk large carving axe. An excellent all-round carving axe with convex bevel. Right: Hans Karlsson slöjd axe with a flat over hollow grind, my dedicated spoon-carving axe.

CARVING KNIVES

The straight knife, sloyd knife, carving knife, wood-craft knife, or whittling knife is perhaps the most accessible tool in the spoon carver's tool kit. The multitude of different knives available today can be confusing, but the temptation to 'make do' with a pocket knife or bushcraft knife with a secondary bevel will lead to unsatisfactory results. Opinel knives and Swiss Army knives are wonderful in their own applications but are not designed for spoon carving. Their short secondary bevel is too obtuse to 'slice' and leave a clean finish on the wood in the way a Scandinavian bevel can.

The following factors should be considered when choosing straight blade knives:

- The maker
- The steel used
- Forging and heat treatment
- Bevel grind
- Dimensions of the knife: edge profile, length of cutting edge
- Handle: dimensions, wood choice
- Sheath

There are a wide variety of carving knives available today, the majority of which have between a 25-degree bevel and 28-degree flat over hollow or zero Scandi grind. A flat bevel is key for carving as the bevel has been ground at an efficient angle which guides the entire blade through the cut in a slicing motion. Blades with secondary bevels or micro bevels require a steep angle and bite into, rather than slice through, the wood.

Table of recommended straight blade knives

Maker	Knife	Country	Steel	Grind
Morakniv (Mora)	Mora 106	Sweden	Carbon	Flat Scandi
Morakniv (Mora)	Mora 120	Sweden	Carbon	Flat Scandi
Hans Karlsson	Slöjd knife	Sweden	Carbon	Flat/hollow
Svante Djärv	Slöjd knife	Sweden	Carbon	Flat/hollow
Kay Embretsen	50–90mm sloyd	Sweden	Carbon	Flat/hollow
Nic Westermann	Sloyd knife	UK	Carbon	Flat/hollow
Hewn and Hone	Turning sloyd	UK	Carbon	Flat
Adam Ashworth	90mm sloyd	UK	Carbon	Flat/hollow
Tamarkin	Sloyd knife	Israel	Carbon	Flat/hollow
Aleksander Majcen	80mm slöjd	Slovenia	Carbon	Flat/hollow
Reid Schwartz	95mm slöjd	USA	Carbon	Flat/hollow
Matt White	4in sloyd	USA	Carbon	Flat/hollow
Josh Whitehead	4in sloyd	USA	Carbon	Flat/hollow
Strong Way Tools	Carving knife	Ukraine	Carbon	Flat

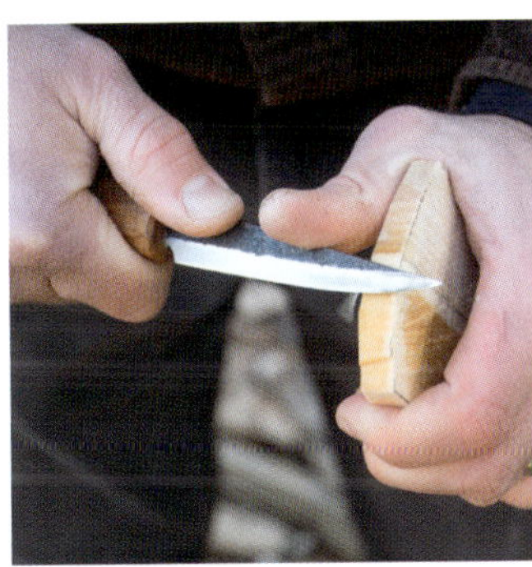

Nic Westermann sloyd knife with flat over hollow grind.

From top to bottom: Nic Westermann sloyd knife, Dave the Bodger finishing knife, Hewn and Hone turning sloyd, Hans Karlsson slöjd knife, Mora 106 carbon and Mora 120 carbon steel.

HOOK KNIVES

Hook knives, also known as crook knives or spoon knives are essential tools for the spoon carver. They are specifically designed for hollowing out spoon bowls. They are wonderful tools, as they liberate the carver from having to use gouges and a workbench. On the flip side they can be hard to get the hang of, and for people with arthritis or finger mobility issues I recommend a combination of gouges or hook knives used in a workbench, vice, clamp or spoon mule.

Hook knives are specialist tools and unfortunately there are a plethora of badly produced hook knives available on the internet that are entirely useless for the purpose of carving spoons!

The following factors should be considered when choosing hook knives:

- The maker
- The steel used
- Forging and heat treatment
- Bevel grind
- Dimensions of the knife: edge profile, length of cutting edge, curve of the blade
- Handle: dimensions, wood choice
- Sheath

There are a variety of different hook knives on the market today. The best examples are hand forged by expert blacksmiths who are also experienced woodcarvers. It is possible to carve with one hook knife and one hook knife only. Buying one high-quality tool is a wiser investment than a cheap one that will soon be blunt, discarded and need to be replaced.

Table of recommended hook knives

Maker	Type	Country
Wood Tools	Compound curve	UK
Wood Tools	Open curve	UK
Hans Karlsson	Hook knife	Sweden
Svante Djarv	Small/standard	Sweden
Nic Westermann	Twca cam/finishing hook	UK
Nic Westermann	Roughing/fawcett/open curve hooks	UK
Aleksander Majcen	Spoon carving knife	Slovenia
Reid Schwartz	Hook knife	USA
Kay Embretsen	Open/standard hook	Sweden
Matt White	Monadnock hook knife	USA
Josh Whitehead	Compound/hook knife	USA
Strong Way Tools	Twca cam/hook knife	Ukraine

'Crook knife', otherwise known as a hook knife, for hollowing a spoon bowl.

Left to right: Svante Djärv small hook knife, Hans Karlsson hook knife, Wood Tools open curve hook knife, Nic Westermann fawcett hook, open curve and roughing hook knife.

Hook knives' dimensions vary in terms of the radius or curvature of the hook and edge profile – from small hooks designed for carving mini scoops and teaspoons, to large twca cams designed for carving spoons, ladles and kuksas.

GOUGES

If you were to ask a traditional carpenter how to make a spoon, they would almost certainly use a bent gouge or spoon gouge in a workbench vice to carve. This is a straightforward way to carve a spoon from seasoned timber and, as mentioned, this can be a beneficial approach for those requiring additional support due to restrictions in mobility, even when carving green wood. The huge benefit and perhaps underrated function of gouges is the ability to remove large amounts of wood with little physical effort as they are available in a range of cranks, sweeps and diameters; they bring larger projects, such as ladles and flour scoops, into reach whilst removing the risk of repetitive strain from axe carving. Clamp the spoon in a workbench, vice, spoon mule or even to your chopping block with a ratchet strap.

Table of recommended curved gouges

Maker	Country	Gouge	Cutting edge length	Sweep
Pfeil	Switzerland	Long bent gouges	5–35mm	5L (shallow) – 8L (curved)
Kirschen	Germany	Curved gouges	4–30mm	Shallow/ curved
Nic Westermann	UK	Swan neck gouges	440–5mm	50–70mm sweep
Ray Iles	UK	Curve gouges	1–25mm	12–20mm sweep
Hans Karlsson	Sweden	Carving gouges	30mm	35mm radius
Svante Djärv	Sweden	Dogleg gouge	25mm	30mm
Strong Way Tools	Ukraine	Doglegs/ curved	Various	Various

Kirschen Tools curved gouges with Beech wood mallet.

Kirschen curved gouges in a range of different 'sweeps'. The sweep is the curve of the cutting edge: the shallower the curve, the shallower the cut; the steeper the curve, the deeper the cut and the more material removed.

To choose one general-purpose curve gouge for spoon carving, a mid- to shallow sweep is recommended, with a cutting edge of 20–25mm.

ADZES

Adzes are brutally efficient tools. They require minimal exertion for maximum outcome. Adzes can be used to 'rough out' large ladles and – with practice – small eating spoons, removing large wood chips with a flick of the wrist.

Adzes are specialist tools and require specific ergonomics to perform as they should. Much like hook knives, there are a few mass-produced adzes available on the market, but to date, I have found none perform their function as well as they could. So too, the majority of vintage adzes today are designed for different applications, such as shipwrights' adzes, coopers' adzes and gutter adzes, and it is rare to find a vintage adze with the correct edge profile for spoon or bowl carving.

However, there are some fantastic hand-forged adzes available.

Table of recommended adzes

Maker	Country	Adze
Hans Karlsson	Sweden	35mm/50mm/60mm adzes
Svante Djärv	Sweden	40mm and 60mm adzes
Oscar Rush	UK	30mm and 50mm adzes
Josh Burrell	UK	35mm and 50mm adzes
Strong Way Tools	Ukraine	Bowl/curved/Finnish adzes

Top to bottom: Oscar Rush 50mm adze, Svante Djärv 45mm adze, Oscar Rush 30mm adze.

Adzes come in a variety of sweeps and edge profiles. Generally speaking, a 45mm adze is the most versatile size for roughing out both large cooking spoons and eating spoons. A 30mm adze can be very effective for eating spoons and small coffee scoops and a 50mm adze will suit bowls, kuksas, ladles and larger spoons.

FINISHING TOOLS

There is a wide variety of finishing tools, which can be used to carve patterns and decoration ranging from chip-carving knives and kolrosing blades to small scorps, gouges and chisels. From texturing to inlay carving and figure carving, the potential for decoration on spoons is seemingly endless. A basic set of chip carving knives can be a great starting point.

Set of Kirschen carving tools, including a straight chisel, V gouge, gouge and three chip carving knives.

Kirschen Tools cranked chip-carving knife.

TOOL CARE

Taking care of your tools will ensure their longevity. Japanese temple carpenters sharpen and store their tools after each and every use. At the end of the year, they place their tools in a tool wrap and thank them for their service. This is the kind of reverence our edge tools deserve.

Carbon steel will rust in the presence of moisture (even in the air). If you aren't using them regularly, a thin coating of linseed oil or tool wax will prevent them going rusty. Storing tools in tool rolls with sheaths is highly recommended to ensure they stay in top condition.

Waxed canvas tool bag by Tobolka Bags, with dedicated tool rolls, provides a secure and durable home for all my edge tools.

TOOLS FOR CHILDREN

Start children whittling young and they can develop into very competent carvers. My son started carving with a potato peeler when he was 3, and with a knife aged 4. Giving children responsibility with edge tools is a core principle at forest schools, as supporting children to take positive risks is empowering and promotes learning and development.

Potato peelers teach the principles of carving away from the body, and can be used to carve the bark off straight lengths of green wood such as Hazel and Willow. There are a variety of safety knives with a blunt rounded tip that children can safely progress onto, but it is essential that children use those that are dedicated carving knives with flat bevels. Rounded tips will prevent puncture wounds, but these knives are still razor-sharp and require supervision and teaching to use effectively. I recommend accessing a children's whittling tutor or local forest school with an experienced teacher. Cut-resistant gloves can be used as an added layer of safety.

Learning the craft of whittling safely.

FIRST AID KIT

A standard household first aid kit is not fit for purpose for dealing with potential injuries from axes, knives, saws and chainsaws. A well-stocked first aid kit should be clearly labelled 'First Aid', ideally in a waterproof and visible container, available at arm's reach at all times and open-able with one hand. It is well worth undertaking a two-day outdoor first aid training course or equivalent and obtaining appropriate chain-saw safety and maintenance qualifications if using a chainsaw.

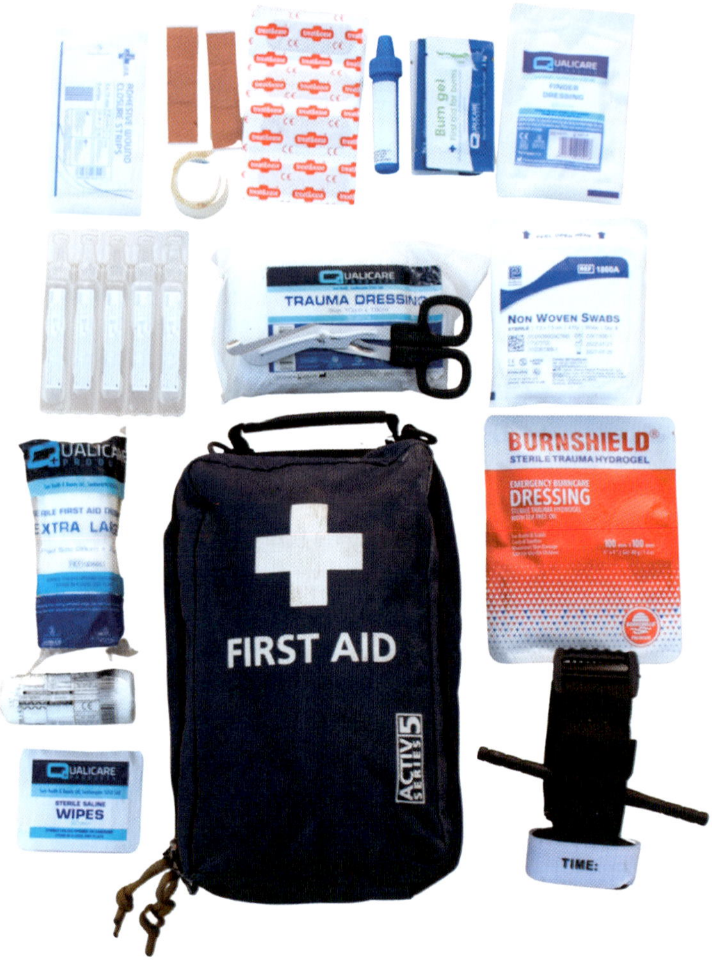

Additional items to add to a standard first aid kit to provide a comprehensive response for dealing with edge tool and chainsaw injuries.

FIRST AID ESSENTIALS FOR EDGE TOOL INJURIES

- 10 × nitrile gloves
- Dressing gauzes
- Sterile cleansing wipes
- 2 × trauma bandages (the 'Israeli bandage')
- 2 × finger bandages
- 6 × steri-strips
- 2 × rolls microporous tape
- 20 × long fabric stretchy plasters
- 6 × sterile 20ml ampoule wound cleansing solution

FIRST AID ESSENTIALS FOR CHAINSAW INJURIES

- 2 × tourniquets (SWAT-T or equivalent)
- 2 × large compressed dressing gauzes
- 2 × WoundClot Trauma 8 x 20cm
- 2 × large haemostatic gauze dressings
- 1 × Pro-Series medical shears
- 1 × mini surgical marker pen

TROUBLESHOOTING AND FAQS

My tools are rusty; how do I remove rust from them?

Place the tool in a vice or clamp to keep it secure, and take care: it may be rusty but still sharp. Scrub rust with a wire brush or steel wool. This will help remove loose rust flakes and surface oxidation. Wire brush fittings can be fitted to drills or angle grinders to speed up the process. Wear protective glasses and gloves, as little pieces of metal are prone to flying off. Tin foil, scrunched up into a rough ball and lubricated with WD40 or Coca-Cola works surprisingly well. So too does submerging the rusted tool in a container filled with white vinegar and letting it soak for several hours – this will help dissolve the rust. A product called Evaporust chemically converts rust into a more stable compound that can be easily removed. It is non-toxic and can be used to soak batches of rusty tools.

How do I prevent my tools from getting rusty?

Wipe down your tools after use with a dry cloth, removing any debris or tannins. The tannins in some woods will stain your edge tools, but this can be cleaned with a metal polish such as Autosol. Keep tools in dry storage with as little exposure to humidity and sunlight as possible. Steel can be given a wipe with a cloth soaked in linseed oil or alternatively coated with a natural tool protection wax for long-term storage.

How often should I oil my tool handles?

The frequency of oiling tool handles can vary depending on several factors such as the type of wood, climate conditions and frequency of use. There is an old adage that a new axe handle should be given a coat of linseed oil once a day for a week, once a week for a month, once a month for a year, and then yearly. Once a wooden handle is thoroughly saturated with oil the wood fibres become blocked with cured oil, preventing shrinking from moisture entering and leaving the handle.

My axe head is loose, what can I do?

Contrary to some advice, chucking it in a bucket of water overnight will not only be insufficient but will make the problem worse. If the handle is in serviceable condition, it is possible to remove the current wedge with a punch or by drilling it out, tapping out the handle and re-hanging the axe with a larger wooden wedge and metal fastener. In most cases, a new handle and a new edge will be required.

Can't I use a DIY hatchet?

A DIY hatchet is designed for splitting firewood and often comes fairly blunt with a badly ground convex bevel. This renders it completely ineffective for spoon carving, as we require a razor-sharp edge with an appropriate edge bevel to carve spoons. The table of recommended axes in this chapter provides a range of options, together with a list of stockists at the end of the book.

I was given a cheap set of spoon-carving knives as a present; how do I tell if they are any good?

The chances are if they weren't made by Mora or by an independent tool maker specialising in spoon-carving tools, they will be made from cheap steel that will go blunt quickly and won't hold its edge. In addition, the edge profile will also be wrong, making them redundant for spoon carving. Do not throw them out, however – they will make ideal practice blades for tool sharpening! The table of recommended tools in this chapter provides a range of options together with a list of stockists at the end of the book.

CHAPTER 3

SHARPENING

You do not rise to the level of your goals. You fall to the level of your systems.

– JAMES CLEAR

Sharpening needn't be a chore, nor is it a dark art. It requires patient practice to get the hang of it, and there are a few basic principles that can help you master what will become a lifelong skill. The satisfaction of having razor-sharp tools is superseded only by the results which they will produce in the spoons they carve. Sharpening may be likened to practising a musical instrument: expect to be a little out of tune at first, but diligent practice, focus and determination will go a long way! It is key to have a dedicated place for sharpening with good lighting and a stable surface to sharpen upon.

It is all too easy to get by with tools that are 'sharp enough', but the chances are they simply aren't as sharp as they could be. Not all tools arrive sharp out of the box – nearly all mass-produced tools require regrinding or tuning up, even when brand new.

Performing the paper test before you start carving will give an honest assessment of the state of all your tools – your carving axe included! As a rule, if your edge tools can't slice through paper, they're not yet up to the task of carving beautiful spoons.

Holding a piece of paper (80gsm or less), slice it at a 45-degree angle, curving the knife as you cut. If the tool catches at any point, there is an inconsistency in the edge and the tool requires sharpening.

The paper test gives a quick diagnosis of sharpness.

KEY IDENTIFIERS OF SHARPNESS (KIOS)

The Key Identifiers of Sharpness (KIOS) checklist enables us to diagnose if a tool is sharp. Check your edge with an engineer's loupe (10× magnification or more), a magnifying glass or by naked eye.

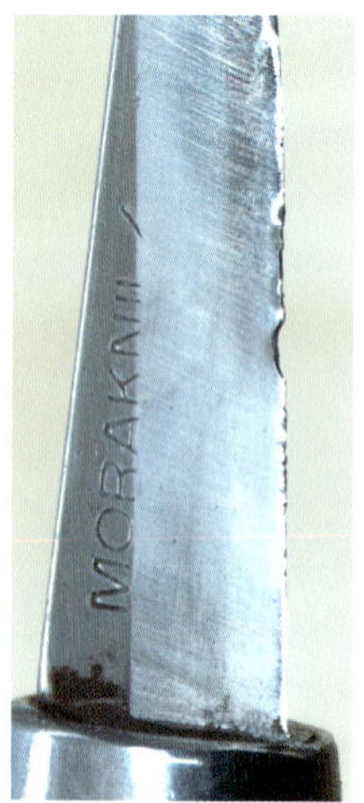

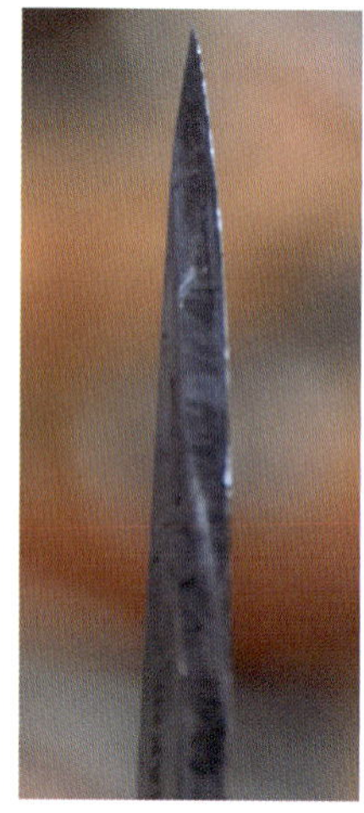

Left: nicks and dents in the edge. This knife needs jointing and sharpening with a coarse grit stone. Right: tiny steel particles along the edge. Tiny steel particles have been displaced and are glinting along the edge – this knife needs to be sharpened, starting with a coarse grit.

An even scratch pattern. The scratch pattern are the grooves in the steel left by the abrasive. On the Mora knife pictured, the scratch pattern is consistent from the back of the bevel all the way to the edge of the blade.

Appropriate and consistent bevel angle. The angle of the bevel should be consistent to the edge of the tool. Here the centre of the knife's bevel has been 'hollow ground' and the two rails at the back of the bevel and the edge are flat, making it easy to sharpen as there's less steel to remove.

Splitting fibres: why sharp tools help make beautiful spoons

From the first split of a log with a froe to the last finishing cut with a knife, the entire process of carving a spoon from a log is to engage in the act of fibre splitting, until you have removed all the wood that isn't a spoon. The cleaner the split of the fibres, the better the finished spoon. This applies right from the get-go; a blunt axe will create a rough, uneven outline of a spoon, which will likely set up a cascade of errors and this will show up in the finished spoon.

The sharper the tool, the cleaner the split of each fibre – with razor-sharp tools you will be able to execute the spoon design of your choice without secretly reaching for sandpaper to abrade all those rough fibres away!

SHARPENING KIT

A comprehensive sharpening kit provides the ability to restore blunt and neglected tools into razor-sharp carving implements. The kit pictured offers the versatile choice of either diamond stones or waterstones.

When starting out, one set of 400, 600, 800, 1000 and 2000 waterstones, or two double-sided diamond stones (extra coarse/coarse and fine/extra fine) would take care of axe and knife sharpening. I recommend high-quality diamond stones, such as DMT, as they are low-maintenance and efficient. The hook knife sharpening sticks are relatively inexpensive and essential for maintaining hook knives. They vary in size, from 10mm for tighter radius hook knives, 20mm for standard hook knives and 30mm for wide curved gouges and adzes. Stropping compounds are also inexpensive and when mounted on 10mm MDF provide superb cost-effective strops.

Your sharpening system can be built upon over time. Hones such as the 20,000 grit Welsh slate stone are ideal for maintaining flat over hollow grinds. I keep a small honing stone in my tool bag for keeping my axe edge in shaving-sharp condition. An axe puck is also a worthy investment; so too are a range of bastard-cut, second-cut and smooth-cut metal files for edge restoration. A dedicated base for holding your sharpening stones is also advisable.

I would not recommend buying budget diamond stones, as they will cut steel well for a few weeks and then wear out, whereas high-quality diamond stones will last for thousands of sharpens. Ultimately, you get what you pay for. Focus on high quality coarser stones as they do the most work, and then build your kit as your appetite for scary sharp tools increases.

Sharpening kit flat-lay. From left to right: Autosol metal polish; Bahco bastard cut file; DMT double sided extra coarse/coarse diamond stone on DuoSharp Base; three small DMT diamond stones (coarse, fine, extra fine); Welsh slate 20k grit hone with dressing stone; four King Bear Japanese waterstones (400, 800, 1200, 3000 grit) with Nagura stone; pocket Welsh slate honing stone 20k grit; Gränsfors Bruk double-sided axe puck; Fallkniven DC4 diamond/ceramic whetstone; Tormek edge marker pen; eraser; six hook knife sharpening sticks (15mm hardwood dowel, 120, 400, 600, 800, 1000, 2000); hook knife strop (15mm hardwood dowel) with stropping compound; MDF strop with DIALUX coarse stropping compound; MDF strop with DIALUX fine stropping compound.

Sharpening kit on a budget

It is possible to put together a sharpening kit for the fraction of the cost of top range sharpening stones. The kit pictured features self-adhesive abrasive film stuck to 10mm acrylic blocks. It is possible to buy sheets or rolls of high-quality abrasive sheets in a range of micron or grits that cut steel very well; however, they do wear out and are therefore a disposable and less eco-friendly option than sharpening stones. For this reason, they are perhaps less economical in the long run but provide a short- to medium-term solution.

Lapping film and microfinishing films

PSA (pressure-sensitive adhesive) lapping films are micron graded silicon carbide or aluminium oxide mineral adhesive sheets. They are extremely effective and are used by professional gem cutters and tool makers alike. They are available in a wide range, from coarser grades (40 micron/400 grit) up to very fine grades (0.25 micron/60,000 grit) used for polishing sapphire and other hard materials.

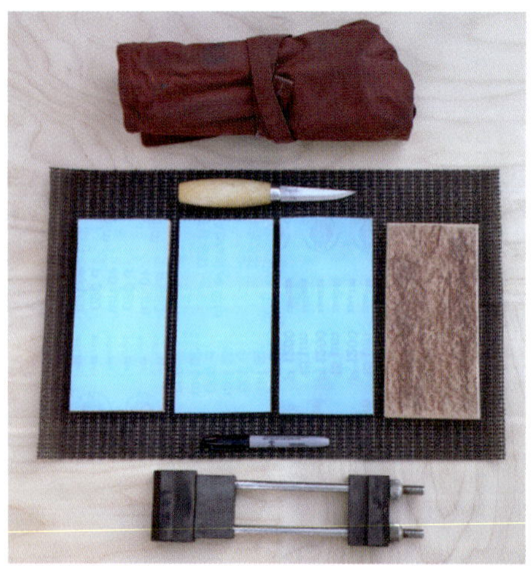

Sharpening kit on a budget.

Lapping films should be applied to extremely flat surfaces, ideally a certified flat granite block or 10mm float glass plate. The surface should be cleaned with white spirit to remove adhesive and must be kept free of scratches or wear. The sheets themselves do lose their adhesive properties if unstuck; a sheet of baking paper will help prolong their stick whilst not in use.

Reconditioning natural sharpening stones

It is possible to restore old oil stones or waterstones which are in reasonable condition and free of large chips or cracks – this chapter will cover how to flatten and maintain natural sharpening stones.

CHOOSING ABRASIVES

Abrasives can be graded in a confusing fashion. Simply put, 'grit' refers to the size of particles embedded in an abrasive material: the higher the grit, the finer the abrasive. However, there are different standards for grit used by manufacturers and grit is therefore not the most accurate of measurements. 'Mesh' refers to the number of evenly spaced holes in a screen per square inch, and a micron (0.001mm) is a unit used to measure the size of particles in an abrasive material.

Micron is therefore the most relevant measurement for our purposes, whilst most people are familiar with the different grits of sandpaper. Although mesh, micron and grit vary between brands the table below should help provide a guide to select the appropriate grade of abrasive. It provides a rough estimate of the approximate grit/micron ratio and includes DMT's colour codes as reputable manufacturers of diamond stones.

Grit, micron and mesh conversion table

Abrasiveness	DMT Colour Code	Approximate Grit	Micron	Mesh	Description
Extra–extra coarse	Silver	150	120	120	Extreme repair of a very damaged edge, used for jointing or re-profiling edge tools.
Extra coarse	Black	300	60	220	For aggressive removal of metal on damaged edge tools. The starting point for restoration of blunt edges and the removal of large chips or dents.
Coarse	Blue	400	45	325	Rapidly sharpens cutting tools or restores a blunt edge. The starting point for most sharpening.
Fine	Red	600	25	600	Ideal for putting a sharp edge on a blade that is regularly maintained.
Extra fine	Green	2000	9	1200	Polishes and refines the edges of fine knives and precision tools after they have been sharpened on coarser grits.
Extra–extra fine	Tan	7000	3	8000	Extra fine polish to an extremely sharp 'razor' edge.

SHARPENING CARVING KNIVES

A dedicated carving knife offers three tools in one: the straight edge nearest the handle for planing cuts, the curved belly of the knife for hewing cuts and the box of the knife for turning cuts. To start out I recommend breaking down the sharpening process into these three sections of the knife.

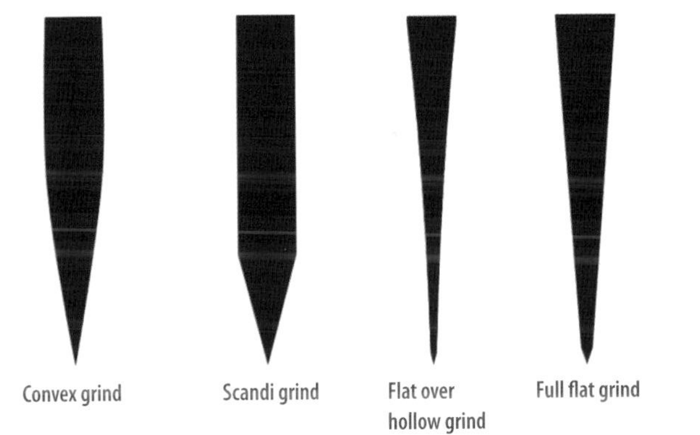

Bevels diagram. Colouring in the bevel with a marker pen enables you to see *exactly* where you have removed steel from the bevel. This is critical when you are starting out, as it helps take the mystery out of the sharpening process.

SHARPENING A CARVING KNIFE WITH A BENCH-STONE

Repeat steps 1 to 7 on higher grits. A good scale of grits to work through sharpening would be 300, 400, 600, 800, 1000, 2000, 5000 and strop. At a minimum, 400, 600, 800, 1000 and strop will take a knife with minor dinks and imperfections to razor-sharp.

Select the appropriate grit sharpening stone from the table on page 55. If in doubt, choose the coarser stone. Place on a flat, sturdy work surface. We will begin by sharpening the 2cm of straight bevel nearest the handle.

Colour in the entire width of the bevel with a permanent marker on both sides.

Lay the spine of the knife flat on the stone. Now tilt the blade onto the stone until the bevel is 'engaged' on the stone. Your fingers will now act as a clamp to maintain this angle as you push the knife across the stone – this is crucial, as even a slight roll of your wrist can result in blunting the edge.

With steady, even pressure, push the knife away from you to the end of the stone. Start by sharpening in one direction. This will help build muscle memory and minimise errors. It is useful to count the number of passes you make – don't be convinced ten or even twenty passes will suffice! The numbers are irrelevant here; the tool is only sharp when we achieve all the key identifiers of sharpness (KIOS, *see* page 52).

Turn the knife over, apply marker pen and repeat on the other side of the bevel. This time the knife will be drawn towards the body with a pull stroke. Pay close attention to achieving an even scratch pattern at all times.

Move along the bevel 2cm and sharpen the belly of the knife. The belly is slightly curved; follow the curvature by moving the knife in a sweeping motion from the middle of the stone to the top corner of the stone. Repeat on the other side.

Move along to sharpen the tip of the knife. To engage the tip of the bevel, the blade must be tilted upwards by lifting the wrist. Depending on the blade, the angle can be quite obtuse; pushing the tip with two fingers on the back of the spine helps push the tip through an arcing motion towards the end of the stone. Repeat on the other side.

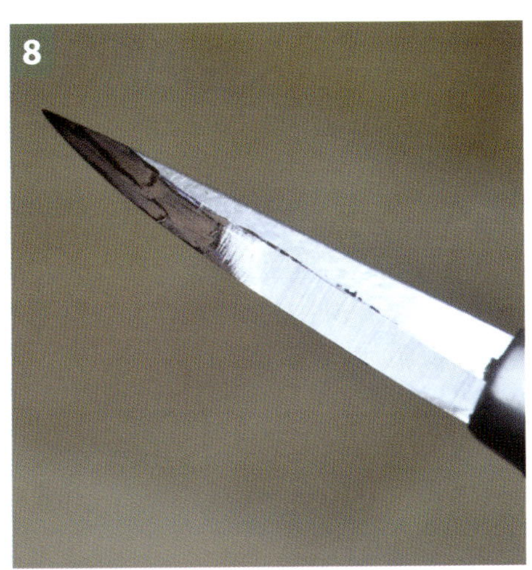

Repeat until you achieve a burr along the entire edge. A burr is the accumulation of abraded steel particles along the edge of the knife, it looks like tiny fuzzy steel crumbs, or a fine wire along the edge. Invest the most amount of time in the coarse grit first before progressing onto a higher grit stone.

Stropping the knife. Stropping technique follows steps 3–7, with the exception that the tool is pulled across the surface of the strop rather than pushed. Stropping compound is abrasive and polishes the steel at a microscopic level, removing the burr and polishing the edge bevel.

The paper test will reveal any inconsistencies in the edge. This knife cut the paper well until the tip where resistance was felt in the paper. A close-up inspection reveals tiny inconsistencies in the edge that need to be sharpened out.

STROPPING

Western cowboy films have given stropping a bad name. Stropping on a leather belt is not advisable for dedicated carving tools. The majority of leather strops are supple and as the edge passes over the surface, the leather 'gives', subtly rounding the edge of the tool. This is known as micro-convection. A micro-bevel can be desirable in some instances, such as on all-purpose bushcraft knives that take a lot of hard use, as it is an inherently strong grind which is easy to maintain.

However, for the purposes of spoon carving, a flat grind is optimal and stropping compound applied to a flat piece of new MDF makes for a cheap and extremely efficient strop without rounding your perfect edge. Stropping is wonderfully effective at maintaining a sharp edge up to a point, but it is no substitute for returning your edge to a good quality sharpening stone.

If there is a slight subtle feeling of resistance at any point the edge requires further fine sharpening. If the paper does not slice at all the tool is very blunt. If, when cutting the paper, it is possible to cut a wavy line without much resistance the tool is sharp and ready for carving.

TROUBLESHOOTING KNIFE SHARPENING

Secondary bevels

Secondary bevels are found on many general purpose and specialist knives, and they have many positive attributes for applications outside of wood carving. However, for precise carving, a 'zero Scandi grind' with a flat 28-degree bevel is desirable.

Removing secondary bevels

It is possible that through sharpening errors a secondary bevel or micro-bevel has been established. Colour in the bevel with a marker pen, then start sharpening on the coarsest grit stone available. The micro bevel should be evident as there will be a black line along the edge of the blade. Continue sharpening until the scratch pattern continues from the back of the bevel until the cutting edge, and you will have successfully removed the secondary bevel. Note that some knives are designed to have secondary bevels, and may not withstand the rigours of carving if re-ground to a flat grind.

The thin light line along the edge of the blade indicates that this knife has a 'micro-bevel' or tiny secondary bevel that will not perform a slicing cut in the way a perfectly flat bevel will.

Altered bevel angle. The bevel angle on this Mora 106 has been altered through incorrect sharpening. The edge is also chipped in multiple places. It will need to be re-ground entirely, ideally using a water-cooled Tormek sharpening system, bench grinder or starting with coarse sharpening stones.

Jointing a knife. Voluntarily blunting a knife may seem counter-intuitive but when a blade edge has significant nicks and dents, or the tip has snapped off, it is necessary to start again and grind a new edge profile. This is the perfect opportunity to establish a new perfectly flat grind by working up the grits from coarse to extra fine.

SHARPENING AXES

A sharp dedicated carving axe is not only a safe axe, but it is extremely efficient and deeply satisfying to carve with. There are two main types of bevel or grinds on carving axes: a flat grind and a convex grind. Flat grinds tend to have a bevel ground between 27 and 30 degrees; convex grinds tend to be ground between 20 and 28 degrees. A bevel gauge is a useful tool for checking the bevel angle on your edge tools, ensuring you maintain correct bevel angles whilst sharpening.

Top: Gränsfors Bruk large carving axe (symmetrical convex bevel). Bottom: Hans Karlsson slöjd axe (flat 30-degree symmetrical bevel). Left: a Veritas brass bevel gauge.

Sharpening a convex bevel

To sharpen a convex bevel on an axe it can be advantageous to use a round axe puck, as a puck lends itself well to making circular abrasions to the steel, which is exactly what we want to achieve when sharpening a convex surface. A small, flat, rectangular sharpening stone or metalworker's file (bastard cut, second cut and smooth files) can also be used.

Clamp the axe in a workbench, vice, or firmly brace it on the edge of a tabletop. Alternatively, the axe can be 'locked' by holding the handle of the axe with your bicep and supporting the head of the axe with your fingers.

Close-up of a symmetrical convex bevel.

Colour in from the heel to the toe along the entire back of the bevel. We will start by sharpening the back of the bevel or 'shoulders' furthest away from the cutting edge.

Place the stone or puck at the back of the bevel and start by making circular motions, slowly working along the entire length of the back of the bevel. At this point you are not removing any steel from the cutting edge. Do not be tempted to skip this step! It is essential to remove steel evenly from the entire bevel and to maintain a convex bevel angle.

Here a small flat diamond stone is used. Colour in the middle of the bevel and work from heel to toe across the entire bevel. Lock your wrist and forearm so your arm becomes an extension of the stone. If you skip steps 2 and 3 and go straight to sharpen the edge, over time you will effectively blunt the axe by creating an acute convex bevel which will not slice into wood – it will become like a splitting axe!

Reapply marker pen to the edge of the bevel and sharpen along the length of the cutting edge. Listen carefully for the tone change: the sound the stone and steel produce goes up in pitch as you sharpen the cutting edge. Do not allow your stone to 'roll over' the edge. Repeat Steps 2–4 on both sides.

The circular motion of an axe puck on a convex bevel will create a scratch pattern that looks like this. With extensive sharpening on certain steels, a burr will have formed; with lighter sharpening a burr is not always evident. Check KIOS to be certain that the bevel is sharp. Repeat steps 2–4 through grits 400, 600, 800, 1000, 2000 or coarse, medium, fine, extra fine.

Strop. Stropping the axe is part of the de-burring process. As with the knife, strop by pulling the axe across the surface of the strop. Start by stropping the shoulders and then gently raise the angle of the axe head to strop all the way to the cutting edge.

Left: convex bevel before sharpening. Right: convex bevel after sharpening, stropping and treating with tool wax for protection against rust.

Sharpening a flat bevel

A flat 'Scandi' bevel can be sharpened in a similar manner as a Scandinavian grind or flat grind on a carving knife. An axe puck, file or sharpening stone can be used. Either clamp the axe in a vice or workbench or to a tabletop, or place the stone itself in a bench-top base. Recommended grits are 400, 800, 1000, 2000 and strop. Flat over hollow grinds can also be sharpened in this method, though will likely require starting on a less coarse grit, depending on the condition of the edge. Apply marker pen along the entire length and width of the bevel and start by sharpening the first 2–4cm closest to the toe of the axe.

Lay the cheek of the axe flat on the sharpening stone and tilt the blade until the bevel is 'engaged' with the stone. Only approximately 2cm of the bevel will actually be engaged with the stone. Push with steady pressure away from you across the stone. Repeat on both sides until a burr has formed.

Continue sharpening the middle and heel of the axe on both sides. An even scratch pattern across the bevel is one of our Key Identifies of Sharpness (KIOS). It is imperative you maintain this angle – even a slight roll of your wrist can result in blunting the edge, apply a little pressure and let the stone do the abrading.

Strop. As with the carving knife, strop by pulling the axe across the surface of the strop. Repeat on both sides. If a strong burr has formed, start with a coarse stropping compound before moving on to a finer finishing compound.

SHARPENING HOOK KNIVES

Hook knife sharpening system

To date there is not an 'off the shelf' sharpening system that can provide the variety of abrasion required for a razor-sharp hook knife. There are ceramic sharpening rods that provide coarse and medium grit options. However, a custom sharpening system is both affordable and extremely effective.

High-quality abrasive wet and dry sandpaper is widely available in a range of grits from 120 up to 10,000 grit and beyond. Sheets can be cut, wrapped and attached to smooth hardwood dowels with rubber bands. The diameter of the dowel is dependent on the blade of hook knife being sharpened: 10mm or less for smaller hooks with tighter radii, or 12–20mm for larger hook knives.

Hook knife sharpening sticks made from smooth hardwood dowel with 120, 400, 600, 800, 1000 and 2000 grit paper attached and a stropping stick.

HOW TO SHARPEN A HOOK KNIFE

The majority of hook knives can be maintained by sharpening the inside bevel of the knife, whilst the outside bevel is simply stropped. The inside bevel of the hook knife should be either flat or hollow ground and as such is relatively easy to sharpen.

Secure the knife by placing it on a flat wooden block raised up from the worktop or in a workbench or vice. It is essential that the knife is secure and any chance of the knife wobbling is minimised.

Approach Step 8 with diligence. It is possible to undo all your sharpening efforts by rolling your wrists and dulling the now-sharp cutting edge. The outside bevel on hook knives can vary: some hook knives have steep secondary bevels; others have quite pronounced convex bevels; and others have flatter bevels which convex more gently. Once again, marker pen is your ally.

Apply marker pen along the entire inside bevel of the hook knife or along the two rails on a hollow ground knife. Select an appropriate grade of sandpaper: 400 grit is an appropriate grit to start with for thorough sharpening.

Place the sharpening dowel on the inside of the bevel. The dowel should be engaged completely flat to the surface of the bevel. Run the dowel along the inside bevel whilst rotating and keeping it perfectly flat.

Continue until a burr appears on the edge and KIOS are present.

Repeat Step 3 through the higher and higher grits. Start with 400 grit and progress to 600, 800, 1000, 2000. I usually sharpen to 6000 grit at these grades – you need only make a few passes to polish the bevel.

Strop the inside of the bevel in the same way as Step 2. Push the dowel in a spiral motion along the inside of the bevel. Repeat until all burr has been removed and the bevel is highly polished.

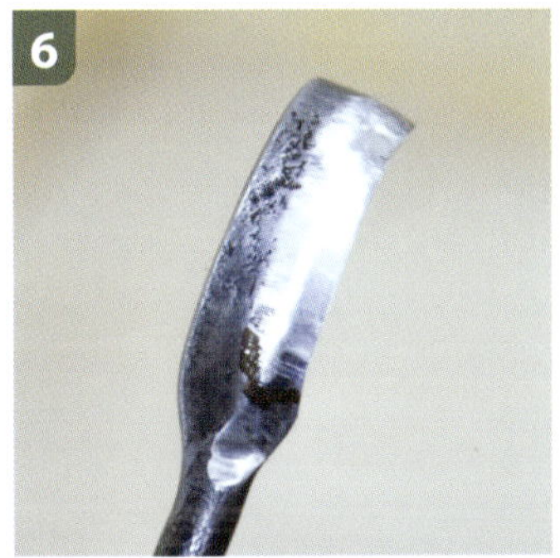

Over time, a wear bevel can start to form, and it is necessary to sharpen the back of the bevel as well. It is possible to skip this step if the back bevel is in good condition.

Sharpen the back of the bevel on a flat sharpening stone, applying the same principles of sharpening a convex bevel – work from the back of the shoulders to the cutting edge in small sections.

Strop the back of the bevel by stropping the shoulders first, then tilting slightly and working towards the cutting edge.

HOW TO SHARPEN ADZES AND CURVED GOUGES

The principles of sharpening adzes and curved gouges are similar to that of sharpening a hook knife. To maintain curved edges, sharpen the inside bevel and when necessary with a wear bevel or when there is edge damage, sharpen the back bevel as well. Both bevels should be stropped regularly.

Raise the tool on a block and sharpen the inside bevel with a sharpening stick or abrasive pad. Repeat sharpening through the grits from 400 upwards to 2000 and as far as your sharpening kit will allow. Follow by stropping the inside of the bevel.

Strop the back of the bevel by moving your hands in an arcing motion – arcing upwards and sideways following the curved, convex bevel. This takes practice; take care not to roll too far.

TROUBLESHOOTING AND FAQS

How do I look after my sharpening stones?

Waterstones and oil need careful maintenance and storage. They are easy to chip and damage, so storing them in a hard case in which they can be easily submerged with water is a good option. With use, waterstones and oil stones will require flattening.

Ensure the paper is on a perfectly flat surface and abrade the stone until all of the criss-cross pattern has disappeared. Your stone is now flat. Neglecting to do this will ultimately 'dish' the stone rendering it concave and not up to the task of sharpening accurately or effectively.

Diamond stones require very little maintenance; however, the build-up of residue will ultimately hinder its abrasive qualities. An eraser can be used to gather up steel particles and keep the stone in good working condition. Adhere to the manufacturer's instructions on whether to use lapping fluid, water or no liquid at all when sharpening.

With a pencil, draw a criss-cross pattern across the surface of the stone, then place the stone face down on a 400-grit coarse abrasive paper or diamond stone.

Restoring hook knives

Jointing a hook knife to remove dents in the edge.

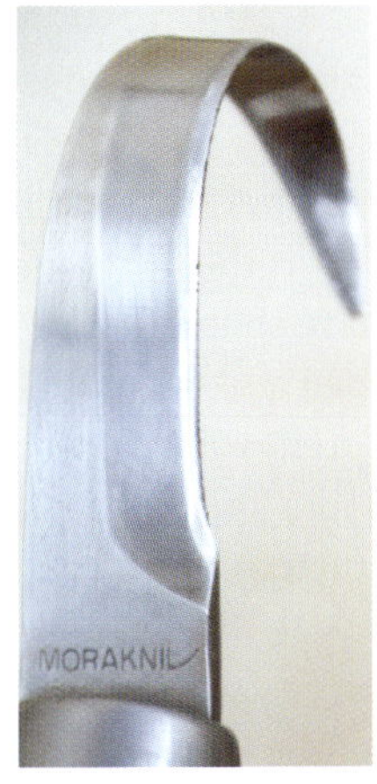

Mora 164 hook knife troubleshooting. Left: rounded outside bevel. Right: rounded inside bevel.

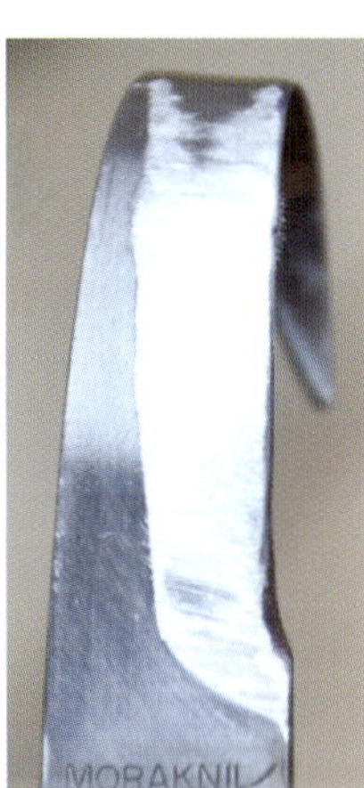

The secondary bevel is coloured black. Right: the secondary bevel is ground away with a coarse abrasive.

Removing chips and dents

If your hook knife has chips or large dinks in the edge it will require jointing to re-establish the correct edge profile. Place the edge of the knife on a sharpening stone, and sharpen the edge down to the bottom of the chip or dent. You now have a blunt but appropriate edge profile. Follow the steps outlined in this chapter to sharpen.

Rounded outside edge bevel

This Mora knife has a rounded secondary bevel. The secondary bevel was originally flat, and the sharpener has rolled their wrist and rounded the bevel. It will require careful attention to reinstate a short flat secondary bevel on a coarse stone. Alternatively, this could be an opportunity to remove the secondary bevel entirely (*see* 'Customising a Mora 164 hook knife' overleaf).

Rounded inside edge bevel

One of the most common errors people make when sharpening a hook knife is rounding over the edge through incorrect sharpening. Often people leave sharpening their hook tool too long, and in the frustration of attempting to get a blunt hook knife sharp again, will neglect to keep the dowel flat against the inside bevel and will unfortunately round the bevel over.

In the photograph above, the marker pen remains in the area in which the bevel angle has changed. The sharpener has rolled their wrist, and the inside bevel is no longer flat. At this point it is possible to re-introduce a flat bevel with continuous sharpening with a coarse 120 grit abrasive paper. To restore the correct flat bevel angle, patience and the reapplication of marker pen is required. You will then be ready to move up the grits to 200, 400, 600, 800, 1000, 2000 and strop.

Customising a Mora 164 hook knife

I am often asked what the cheapest hook knife is on the market today. There are lots of cheap hook tools which are not worth purchasing, as they have poor steel and bad edge geometry. The best entry level hook is the Mora 164; both the pre-2022 and the 2023 models have short secondary bevels that can be challenging to sharpen and maintain. The bevel angle is short and steep and therefore bites into the wood, making it challenging to achieve fine finishing cuts. However, with minor modification the Mora 164 can be turned into an excellent all round hook knife.

The Mora 164 can be customised by removing the secondary bevel on the back of the knife with a grinding wheel or by hand on a coarse sharpening stone. Once there is a continuous bevel from the shoulder of the knife to the cutting edge, you can move from coarser to finer grits, and finally strop.

How can I speed up my sharpening?

Stropping your tools is not a substitute to sharpening, however tools stropped every 15 minutes will hold their edge for extended periods of time. Get into the habit of regularly stropping or returning your tool to an extra fine sharpening stone and you can avoid sharpening for quite lengthy periods of time, provided the tool was razor-sharp to begin with.

However, it is possible to have a highly stropped, highly polished yet blunt tool. Stropping cannot replace sharpening, returning to a grinding wheel or sharpening stone is essential for maintaining the knife appropriately. Using an electric sharpening system, such as a Tormek T-4 or T-8, and maintaining flat over hollow grinds is the preference for many professional wood carvers for speed and efficiency.

USING A TORMEK SHARPENING SYSTEM

A Tormek T-4 sharpening system with dressing stone, edge marker pen, knife jig, hewn and hone jig and bevel gauges.

Setting up the hewn and hone jig. Care must be taken when grinding a Mora knife as the clearance under the jaws of the jig is a matter of millimetres.

Using a marker pen to establish the correct position for introducing a hollow grind to a flat bevel.

Flat over hollow grinds

Don't go hollow grinding your froe! A flat over hollow is more brittle than a flat Scandi or convex bevel but is much easier to maintain.

How often should I sharpen?

This entirely depends on a number of factors, such as how much you carve, the woods you carve, etc. Stropping every 15 minutes will help maintain your knife edge; so too regularly tuning your axe with a very fine stone will prevent the deterioration of your edge. However, it will be necessary to return your tools to coarser abrasives to reinstate correct bevel angles and remove nicks and dents.

If your knife edge glints with little specs of light, it requires sharpening (back to step 1 with a 400 grit abrasive). Similarly, when the knife is leaving scraping marks in the spoon, go back to 400 grit. The longer you leave it the more time you'll need to spend sharpening – so the more frequently you strop and fine tune your edge, the less time you'll spend sharpening a neglected tool.

I seem to be making my edge blunter; why is this happening?

It is likely that your bevel angle has been altered, either prior to sharpening or during sharpening. When pushing too hard on a flat bench stone it is all too easy to roll the wrists and dull the knife. It is also possible that micro-convection has occurred. Use a magnifying glass or loupe to diagnose the problem before going any further.

I have been following instructions, but I still can't get a burr. Why is this?

High quality steels can be very hard, and not all burrs look alike. A burr will readily form if the bevel angle is correct and you are using a coarse grit stone. Check your bevel angle and try using a lower grit sharpening stone when sharpening blunter tools.

Sharpening a flat over hollow grind hook knife is very efficient with very little steel to remove from the 'tramlines' at the back and front edge of the bevel

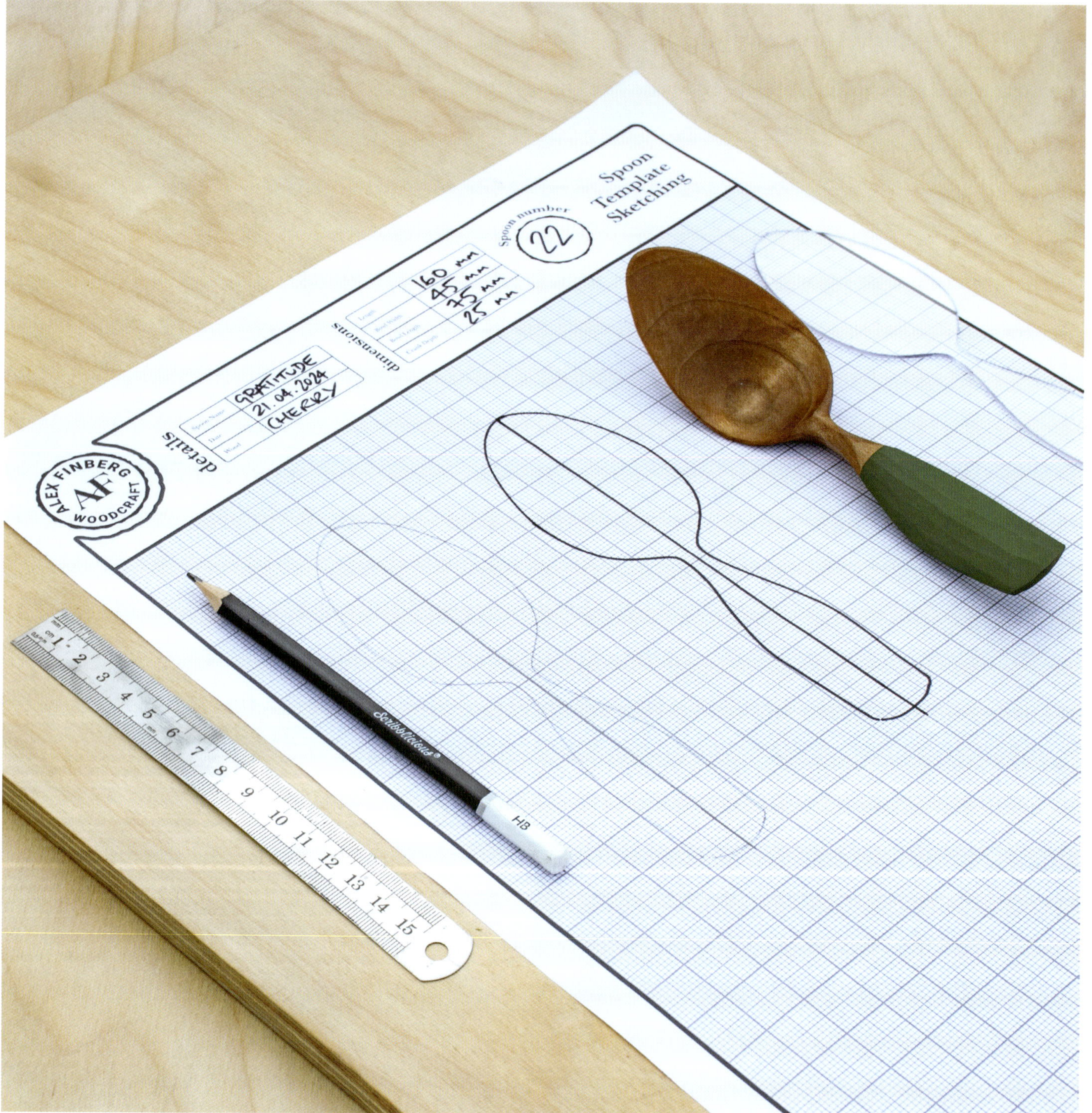

SPOON DESIGN

Compare yourself to who you were yesterday, not to who someone else is today.

– JORDAN PETERSON

It's intriguing to consider that some of the earliest forms of spoons might have been humble sea shells. In the ancient landscape of the Indonesian island of Java, where *Homo erectus* once roamed over a million years ago, archaeologists have unearthed freshwater mollusc shells dating back 500,000 years. What's remarkable is that some of these shells bear evidence of human activity, featuring intricate engravings with zigzag motifs. Around a third of these shells also exhibit precisely drilled holes, likely made using shark teeth, which served to access the mollusc's contents. Could it be that our distant ancestors ingeniously repurposed half a mollusc shell as the very first spoon?

Perhaps we will never know, but what is clear is that the earliest spoon-like utensils were very likely shells and bones, and that *Homo sapiens* didn't start carving spoon-shaped utensils until around the first Agricultural Revolution.

Around 8,000 years ago throughout the Neolithic world, a new type of artefact appeared: small spoons masterfully made from cattle bone. Some of the marks on spoons were made by primary teeth, which indicate their usage in feeding baby gruels to wean infants, the newest innovation in prehistoric baby-care.

The use of carved wooden spoons can be traced back to indigenous cultures who were carving intricate and functional spoons from wood as it had many advantages over other materials, being readily available and lightweight. These wooden spoons were ideal for stirring, mixing and serving food and, due to the abundance of wood, were easily made and replaced.

The word 'spoon' in its current definition is 'an implement consisting of a small, shallow oval or round bowl on a long handle, used for eating, stirring and serving food'. The origin of the word can be traced back to the fourteenth century, from the Proto-West Germanic *spanu*, the Proto-Indo-European *speh*, and from Old English *spōn* ('sliver, chip of wood, shaving').

A collecting of eating spoons.

CULTURAL SIGNIFICANCE

As human societies developed, so did the wooden spoon's cultural significance. In many regions, wooden spoons became associated with tradition, craftsmanship and culinary heritage. Families would often pass down heirloom spoons from one generation to the next, symbolising the continuity of culinary knowledge and the importance of shared meals. In various cultures, the wooden spoon took on ceremonial and symbolic roles. For example, in Scandinavian countries and mainland Europe, a wooden spoon was traditionally presented to a couple on their wedding day, symbolising good luck, fertility and the start of a prosperous life together. Similarly, in certain indigenous communities, elaborately carved wooden spoons held spiritual significance, representing a connection to the land and ancestors, and performed symbolic functions in rituals and ceremonies.

A collecting of cooking spoons.

FORM AND FUNCTION

Wooden spoons also became intertwined with culinary customs and regional dishes. In different parts of the world, specific types of wooden spoons were crafted for specialised tasks. For instance, long-handled wooden spoons were designed for stirring soups in large pots, while intricately carved spoons with flat edges were used for shaping dumplings or pasta. In Chinese cuisine, a wooden wok spatula, resembling a large spoon, is essential for stir-frying and tossing ingredients. In Japanese cuisine, a wooden rice paddle or *shamoji* is used to handle and serve rice, ensuring each grain is delicately handled.

SPOON DESIGN

There are a few key principles to adhere to when carving a wooden spoon. These include carving the appropriate dimensions, including the overall length, length and depth of spoon bowl, handle length and width, and the depth of the crank. To carve a good spoon requires carving in three dimensions, and considering the planes and profiles of the spoon and how they interact.

Unlike carving a flat spatula, carving a spoon is therefore quite complex! Like all creative projects, it helps enormously to sketch a spoon on paper and to potentially use a spoon template to get started.

When carving I follow a mixture of freehand carving and carving to templates, depending on the nature of the spoon. I tend to use templates to carve 'production' cooking spoons, which are designed to look the same and perform the same function. More personal spoons or creative utensils I will carve freehand. Whether I use a template or not, I always follow the steps outlined in this book, as this is the most efficient distilled process I have for carving spoons of any shape or size.

Approaching spoon design as an architect would approach a new eco-building project, means first going to the drawing board. Sketching the spoon design and creating technical drawings can help overcome the obstacles to achieving symmetrical and asymmetrical designs and really help in the creation of original spoon designs. Sketching onto graph paper can support the development of drawing technique and is a great way to 'journal' the evolution of your spoons' designs.

Drawing your design

Designing your own spoon is a wonderful thing – you can even measure the internal diameter of your mouth and carve the spoon proportions accordingly! When designing a spoon from scratch, it can be challenging to achieve symmetry or asymmetry and sketching your template on graph paper or a spoon design sheet can be immensely helpful. Using 1mm graph paper is particularly useful, as you can count the 1mm squares from your centre line and establish a symmetric bowl and handle.

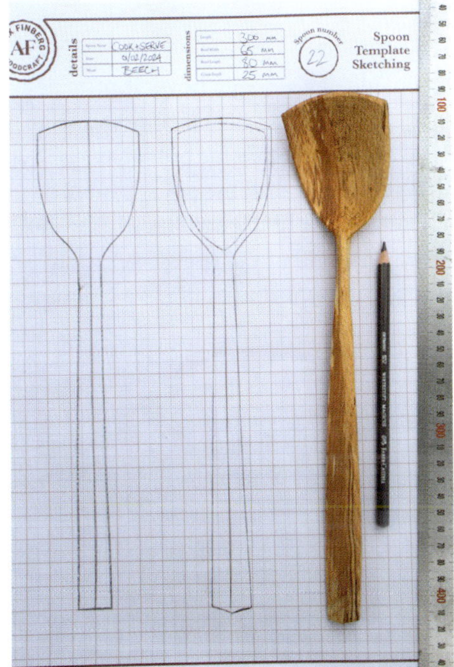

Sketching the cook and serve spoon. The use of design sheets provides the parameters to draw your spoon design creatively. They are a great way to track the evolution of a spoon design and ensure your templates have proportionate dimensions, symmetry and aesthetics.

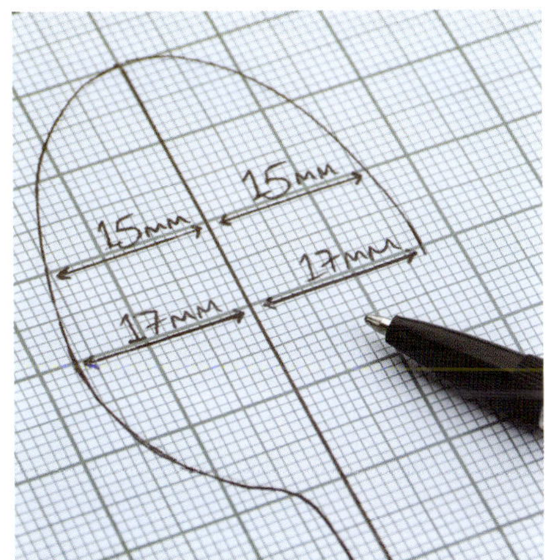

Draw a centre line, then sketch half of the spoon bowl and half of the handle. When you're happy with it, 'mirror' the design and draw the second half of the spoon. Note on this spoon I have gone beyond 15mm on the right-hand side – the eyes can play tricks even when using this precise method!

Templates can be transferred from paper onto recycled plastic sheeting. Trace over the templates in this book with a marker pen onto a piece of recycled plastic, such as milk bottle or file divider, with a permanent marker and cut them out with sharp scissors.

CONTINENTAL CLASSIC EATING SPOON TEMPLATE

Length overall: 178mm

Handle length: 107mm

Bowl length: 71mm

Bowl width: 46mm

Crank depth: 20mm

Copy at 100% scale

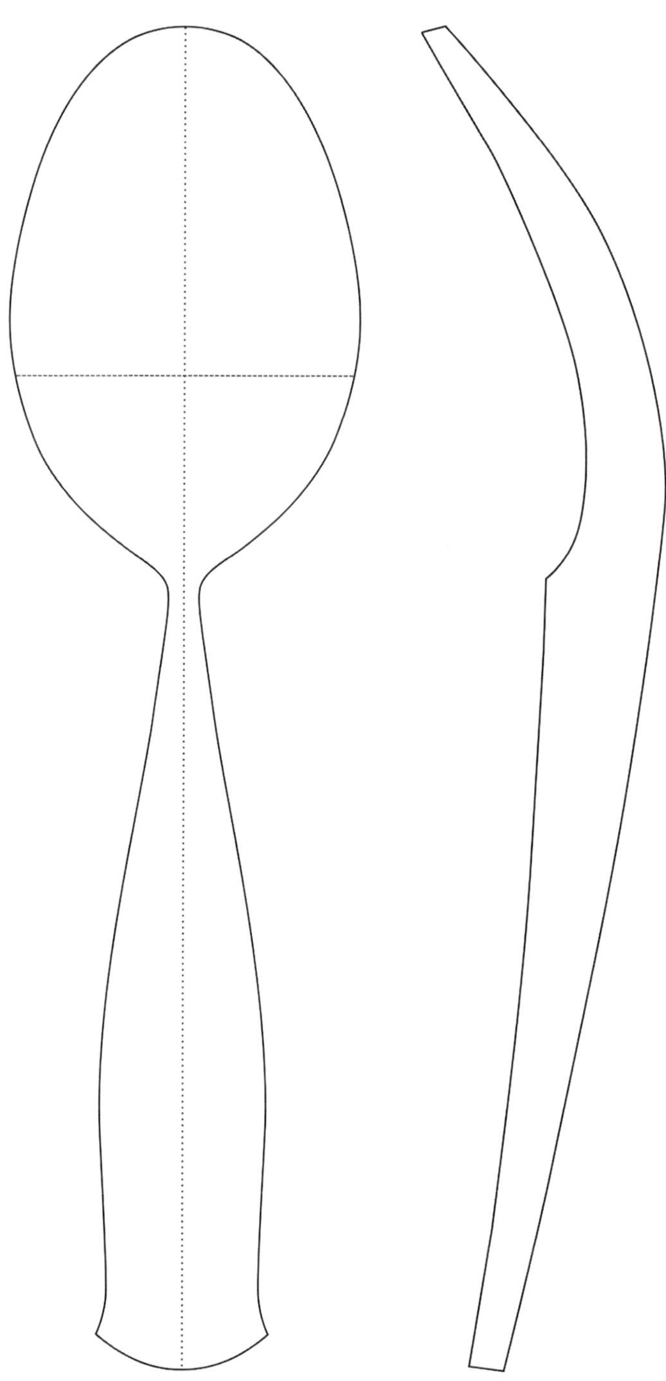

SPOON TEMPLATES

Having an accurate spoon shape to carve to can be invaluable for precise and efficient carving, it removes the majority of issues with symmetry and provides a reliable form to axe carve to. The four eating spoon and four cooking spoon templates in this book are designed to be used and tweaked to your own requirements; they vary from simple symmetric shapes to more challenging ovate forms. The handles can be mixed and matched and the bowls can be shrunk or enlarged to your desired proportions.

To trace a template, upcycle the plastic from old document wallets, milk cartons or yoghurt pots, trace over the spoon outlines with a permanent marker and cut out the template. I keep a wide selection of recyclable spoon templates in a pencil case ready to go.

Eating spoon templates

There are quite a few considerations and design principles to carving a good eating spoon. The proportions of an eating spoon are a matter of taste, unique to the individual. Some enjoy teaspoon-sized bites, while others prefer a larger bowl for shovelling generous mouthfuls. It is crucial to carefully consider the dimensions of an eating spoon to ensure it offers up a slick and satisfying mouthful.

The four templates in the book are some of my favourite shapes to eat with. Each have an aesthetic form I enjoy and fulfil different roles for eating different dishes in different scenarios.

The *Continental Classic Eating Spoon* is the first spoon shape I enjoyed carving repeatedly. It has gone through many evolutions since, and has its origins in Wedding Spoons found in continental Europe. It is used for eating everything.

The *Gratitude Eating Spoon* is a large-bowled eating spoon, which gives a generous mouthful delivered with a short handle. This design fosters a 'hand to mouth' intimacy that is reminiscent of a lineage of Scandinavian spoons going back hundreds of years. It has enough bowl depth for soups and stews.

The *Asymmetric Eating Spoon* is a dainty right-handed eating spoon; the bowl edge has been squared off to a point for scraping food around the inside of a wooden bowl. It provides a satisfying swooping motion for getting the last morsels from a wooden bowl and is used predominantly for porridge.

The *Pocket Shovel Eating Spoon* is a robust pocket spoon ideal for carrying in a pocket, bag or lunch box. Its sturdy handle and shovel-shaped bowl ensure that the spoon can stand up to wear and tear and is perhaps most at home in a children's lunch box.

Eating spoons carved from different woods using the template.

CONTINENTAL CLASSIC EATING SPOON TEMPLATE

Length overall: 178mm

Handle length: 107mm

Bowl length: 71mm

Bowl width: 46mm

Crank depth: 20mm

Copy at 100% scale

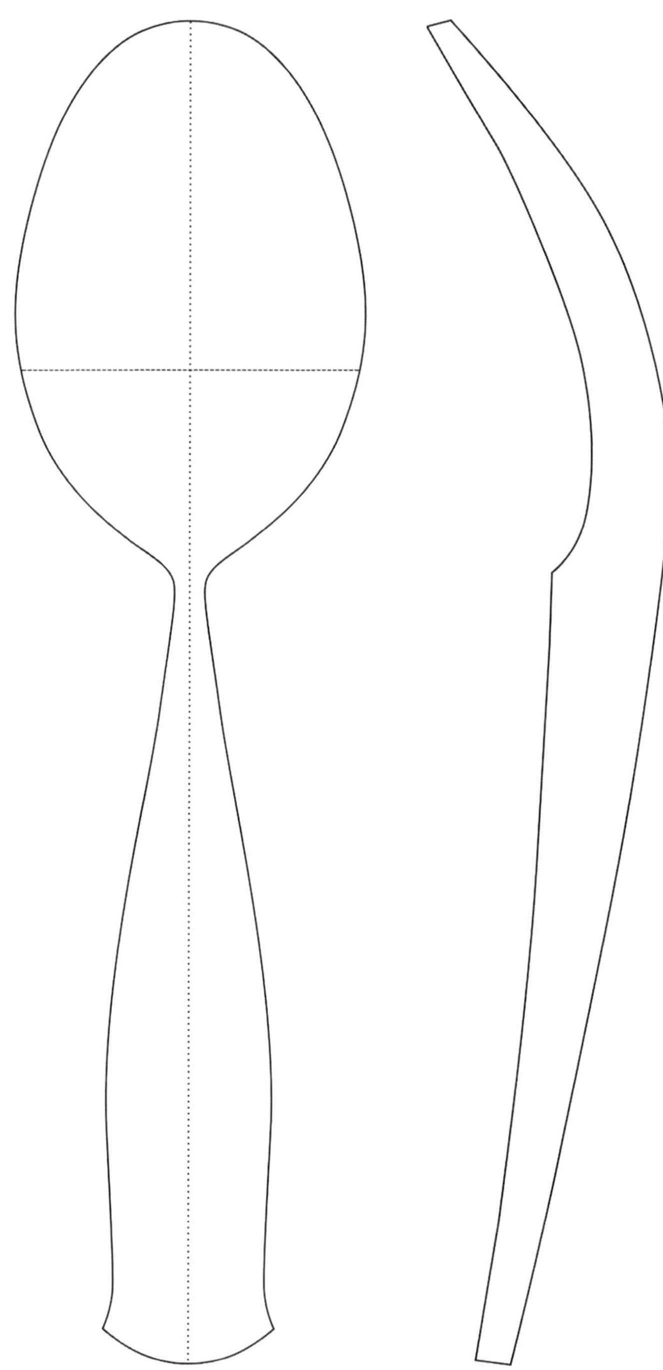

Top profile: *Continental Classic Eating Spoon.*

3D profile: *Continental Classic Eating Spoon.*

Side profile: *Continental Classic Eating Spoon.*

End profile: *Continental Classic Eating Spoon.*

GRATITUDE EATING SPOON TEMPLATE

Length overall: 162mm

Handle length: 84mm

Bowl length: 78mm

Bowl width: 48mm

Crank depth: 25mm

Copy at 100% scale

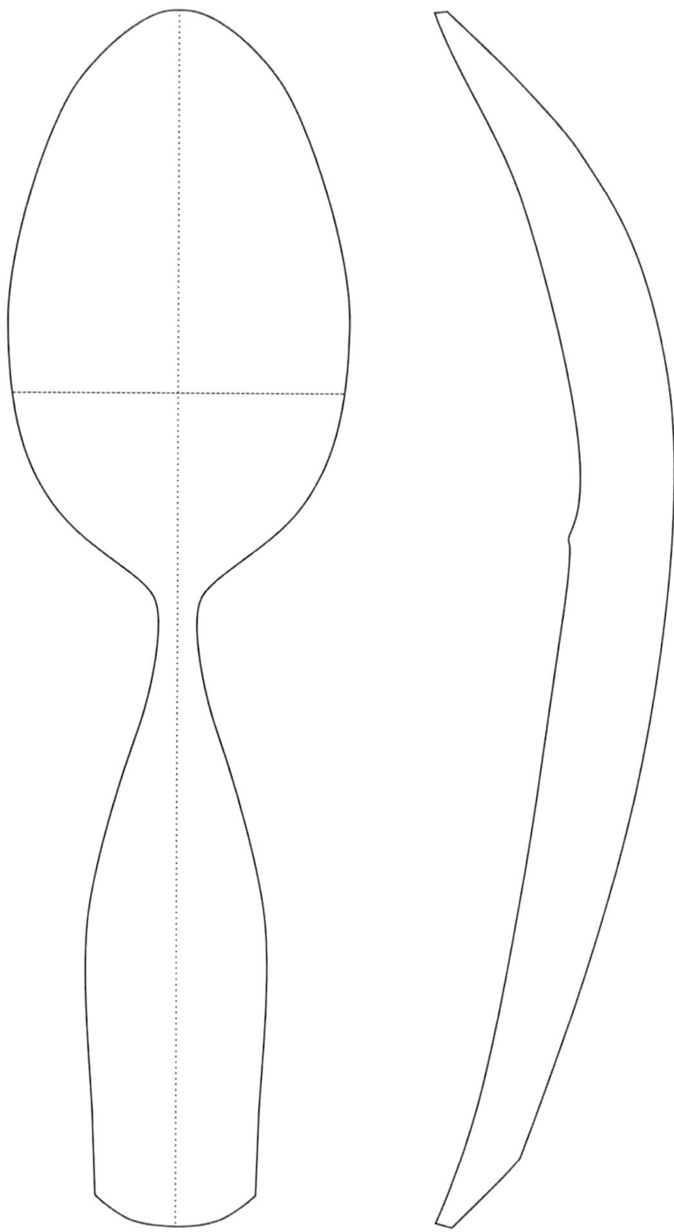

Top profile: *Gratitude Eating Spoon.*

3D profile: *Gratitude Eating Spoon.*

Side profile: *Gratitude Eating Spoon.*

End profile: *Gratitude Eating Spoon.*

ASYMMETRIC EATING SPOON TEMPLATE

Length overall: 158mm
Handle length: 94mm
Bowl length: 64mm
Bowl width: 43mm
Crank depth: 25mm
Copy at 100% scale

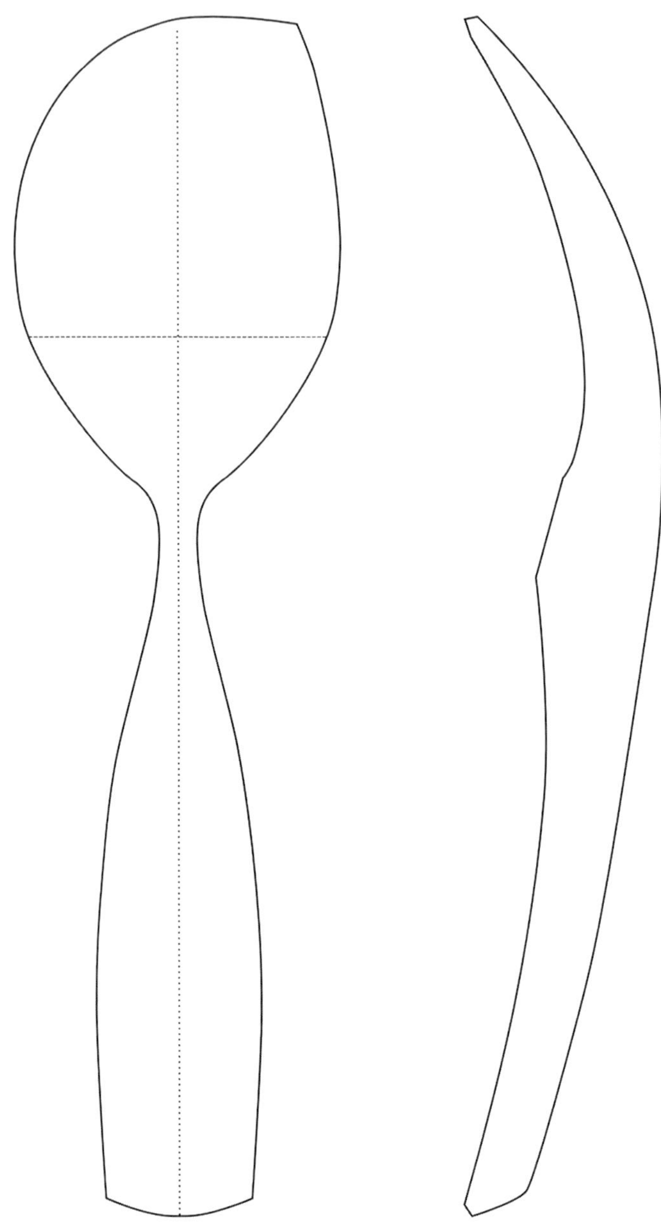

Top profile: *Asymmetric Eating Spoon.*

3D profile: *Asymmetric Eating Spoon.*

Side profile: *Asymmetric Eating Spoon.*

End profile: *Asymmetric Eating Spoon.*

POCKET SHOVEL EATING SPOON TEMPLATE

Length overall: 152mm
Handle length: 90mm
Bowl length: 62mm
Bowl width: 42mm
Crank depth: 25mm
Copy at 100% scale

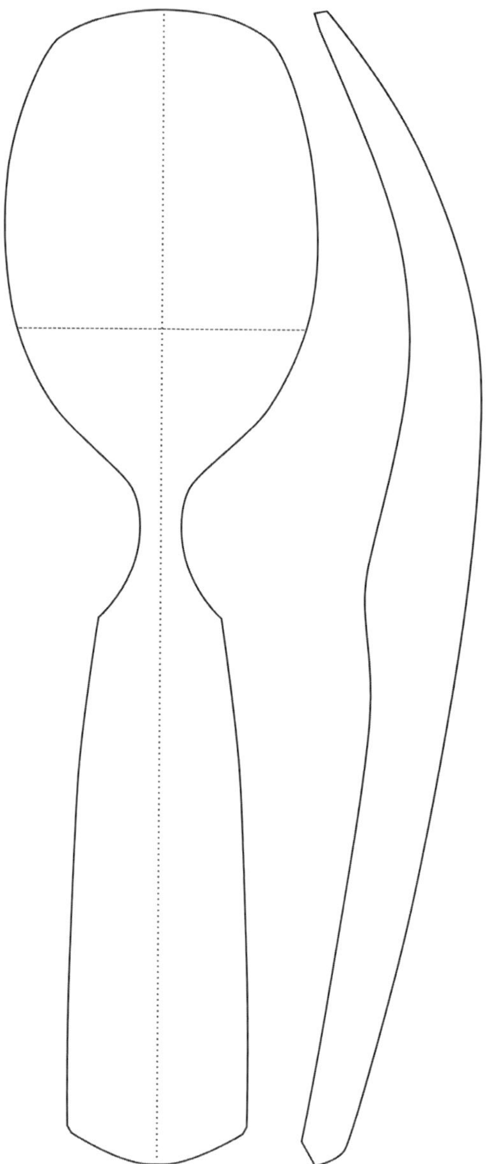

Top profile: *Pocket Shovel Eating Spoon.*

3D profile: *Pocket Shovel Eating Spoon.*

Side profile: *Pocket Shovel Eating Spoon.*

End profile: *Pocket Shovel Eating Spoon.*

COOKING SPOON DESIGN

Cooking spoon designs can be principally governed by functionality, robustness and aesthetics.

Hand-carved cooking spoons can far outlast mass-produced cooking spoons machined from Pine and Bamboo, which tend to have generic shapes. The beauty of carving your own cooking utensils is they can be made to suit the dishes you cook and serve up.

The *Asymmetric Cooking Spoon* is a large-bowled cooking spoon with a squared off rim and pointy edge for scraping the bottoms and corners of pans. The leading edge is left wide to stand up to the rigours of heavy use. This design has been road tested in catering kitchens and is designed to last!

The *Cook & Serve Spoon* is a versatile and elegant spoon. It is perhaps the most reached for shape in my kitchen and as the name suggests it is used for cooking and serving. This shape is extremely versatile: shrink the bowl and it makes a dainty jam spoon, lengthen the handle for cooking in large pots, make a pair into salad servers – the possibilities are endless!

The *Two Penny Cooking Spoon* is a small asymmetric cooking spoon that gets its name from a two-penny coin, which gives a perfect size for getting through the neck of small jars, the pointy tip providing a useful morsel scraper. It is also surprising how useful small bowled cooking spoons are for stirring pots. This design can be enlarged to a full-sized cooking spoon to great effect.

The *Leaf Cooking Spoon* takes inspiration from the ovate leaves of the Devon Whitebeam tree – which amazingly can reproduce without fertilisation, creating seeds that are genetic copies of itself – the perfect spoon shape to be reproduced! The pointy tip of the bowl makes this a favourite all-round cooking spoon.

Cooking spoons carved using the template.

ASYMMETRIC COOKING SPOON TEMPLATE

Length overall: 300mm

Handle length: 201mm

Bowl length: 99mm

Bowl width: 68mm

Crank depth: 28mm

Copy at 100% scale

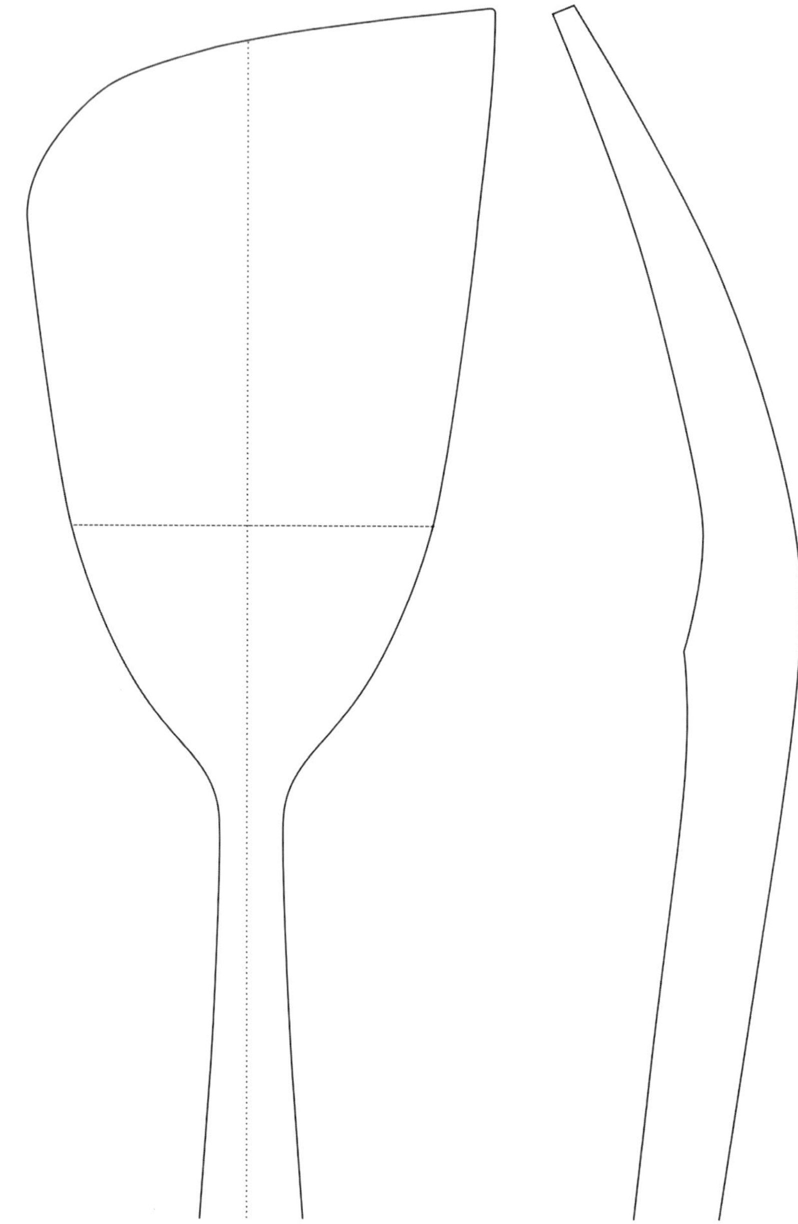

Top profile: *Asymmetric Cooking Spoon*.

3D profile: *Asymmetric Cooking Spoon*.

Side profile: *Asymmetric Cooking Spoon*.

End profile: *Asymmetric Cooking Spoon*.

COOK & SERVE COOKING SPOON TEMPLATE

Length overall: 300mm
Handle length: 230mm
Bowl length: 70mm
Bowl width: 58mm
Crank depth: 20mm
Copy at 100% scale

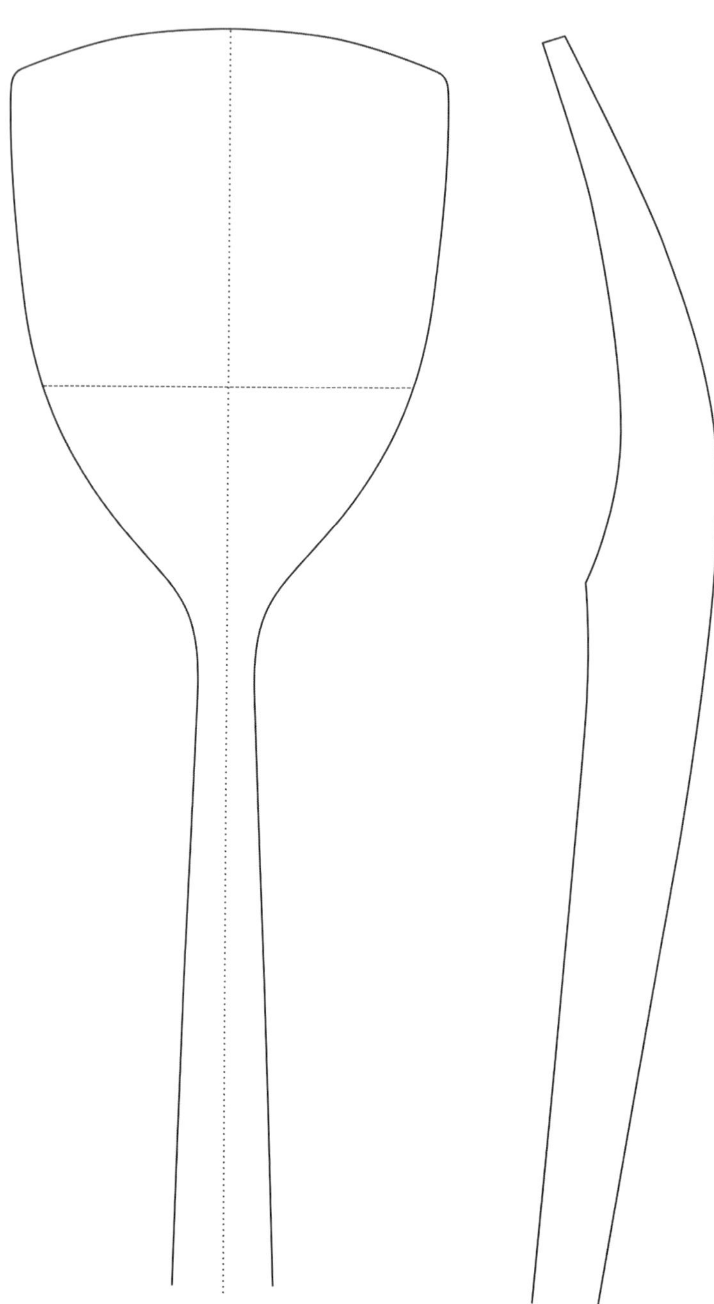

Top profile: *Cook & Serve Cooking Spoon.*

3D profile: *Cook & Serve Cooking Spoon.*

Side profile: *Cook & Serve Cooking Spoon.*

End profile: *Cook & Serve Cooking Spoon.*

TWO PENNY COOKING SPOON TEMPLATE

Length overall: 275mm

Handle length: 230mm

Bowl length: 45mm

Bowl width: 40mm

Crank depth: 20mm

Copy at 100% scale

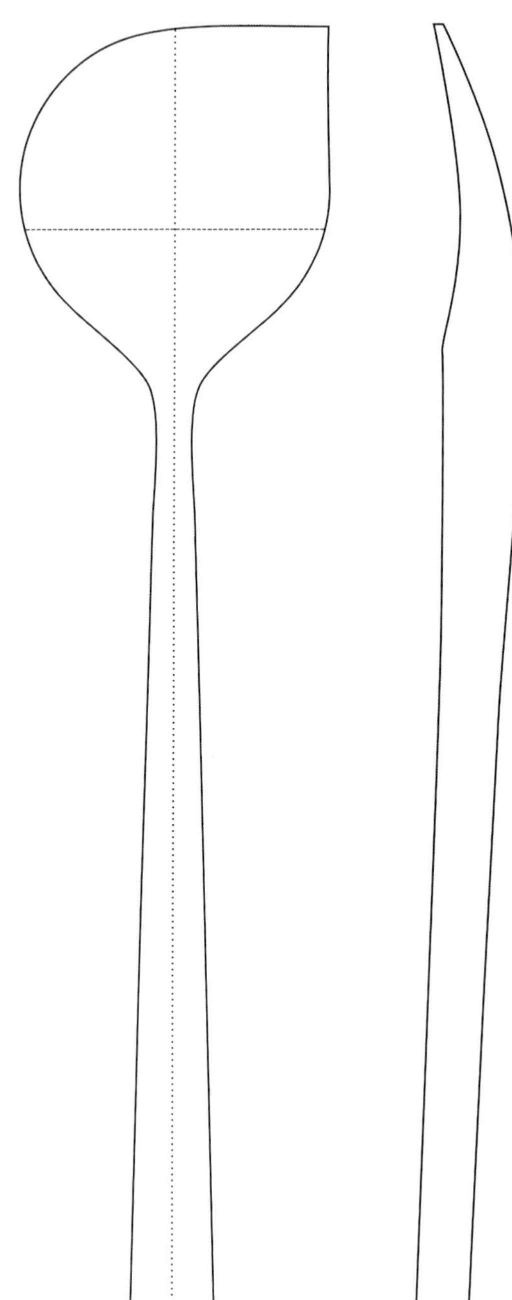

Top profile: *Two Penny Cooking Spoon*.

3D profile: *Two Penny Cooking Spoon*.

Side profile: *Two Penny Cooking Spoon*.

End profile: *Two Penny Cooking Spoon*.

LEAF COOKING SPOON TEMPLATE

Length overall: 285mm

Handle length: 215mm

Bowl length: 70mm

Bowl width: 43mm

Crank depth: 20mm

Copy at 100% scale

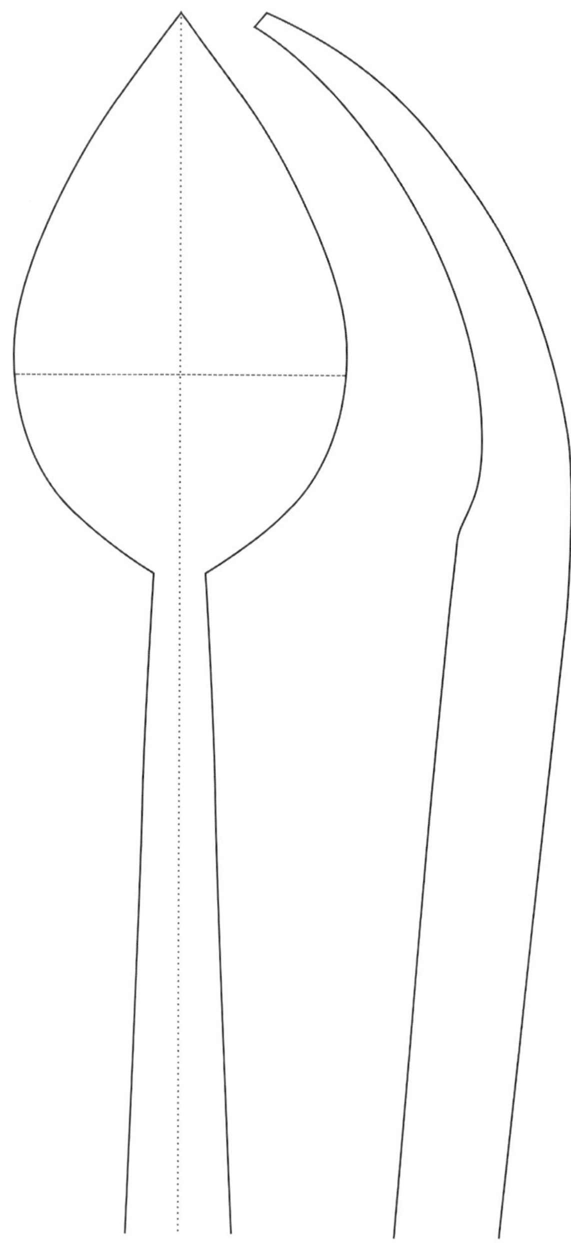

Top profile: *Leaf Cooking Spoon*.

3D profile: *Leaf Cooking Spoon*.

Side profile: *Leaf Cooking Spoon*.

End profile: *Leaf Cooking Spoon*.

PRINCIPLES OF SPOON DESIGN

Dimensional carving

When carving a spoon we are carving a three-dimensional form that has many planes. These include the top of the handle, the back of the handle, the sides of the handle, the back of the handle, the spoon bowl front and back, its sides and any facets, chamfers or micro-planes. The planes often feed into each other, such as the neck transition into the back of the bowl. Giving each plane an intentional design and finish provides a recipe for beautiful spoons. (*See* design features in Chapter 9.)

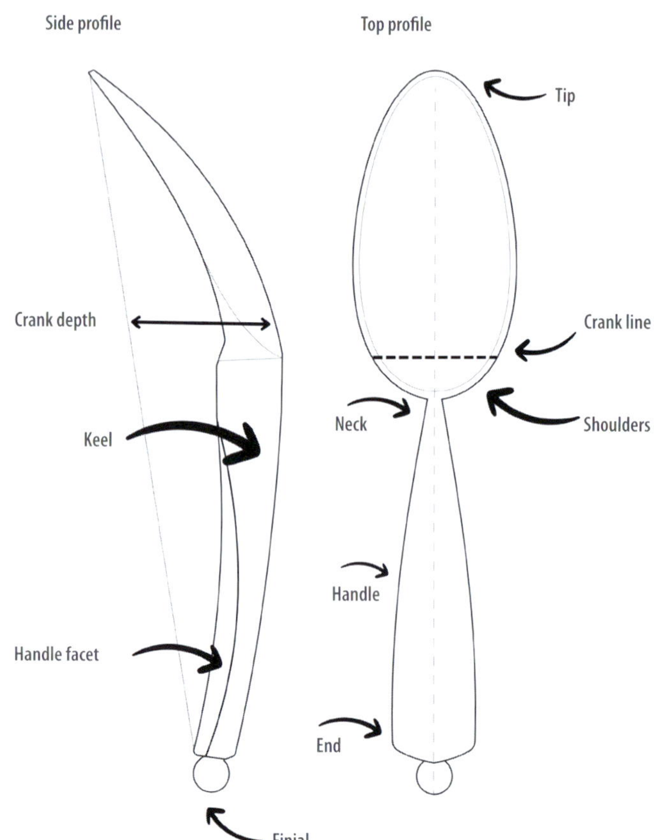

Anatomy of a spoon.

Crank

The 'crank' is the tick shape or curve in the spoon which makes the spoon both ergonomic and elegant. You can of course carve a completely flat spoon or spatula which will perform perfectly well with no crank, whereas serving spoons and ladles require a really deep crank to enable efficient pouring and serving. 'Crooks' or bent branches have natural crank; nature intended these branches to be spoons.

A standard eating spoon tends to have between 1.5–3cm of crank, whereas a cooking spoon could have 2–6cm of crank, or even more, depending on its size. It is important to consider that putting a large crank in a straight piece of wood (for example, for a ladle) will inevitably mean the neck of the spoon will have 'short grain' – making it inherently weak. This can be mitigated by tilting the orientation of the spoon and ensuring the neck of the spoon has a suitably deep keel.

Top: identifying the position of the spoon in the billet. Bottom: the side profile of the billet, shows the depth of the 'crank' in the spoon.

Bowl gradient

The gradient of the spoon bowl is a critical feature both in the feel and performance of the spoon. If an eating spoon is too deep the bowl rim will catch on the lips, too shallow and it won't hold enough food; the same applies to a cooking spoon. A key self-assessment yardstick for eating spoons is the lips, tongue and mouth test – how does the spoon feel to eat from?

Bowl thickness

The thickness of the spoon bowl is also crucial: too thick and it will be cumbersome; too thin and it will break. Cooking spoons require more material to withstand the rigours of sustained exposure to heat and to liquids.

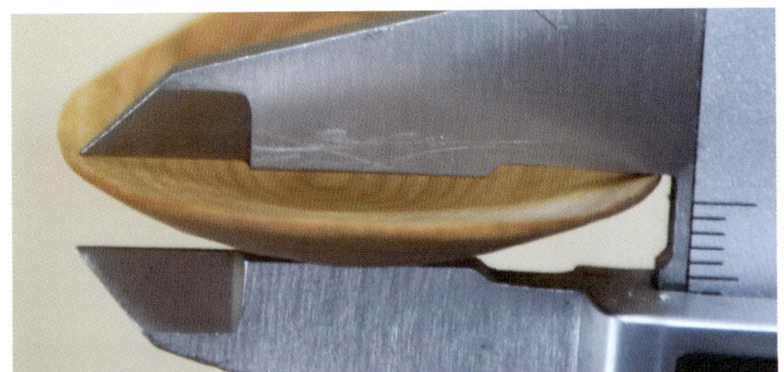

Measuring the gradient of the spoon bowl. This spoon bowl has a gradual gradient with a bowl depth of 4mm at the centre.

This spoon snapped whilst carving. Although the bowl gradient in the inside of the bowl was fine, I carved the back of the bowl too thin (to only 1mm thickness), ignoring the 'wedge principle' – this resulted in the spoon snapping whilst doing the reinforced pull cut.

The wedge principle

The thickness of the bowl is also key both in the structural integrity of the spoon and its functionality. The wedge principle dictates that just like a wooden doorstop, the strength of the tip of the wedge is made possible by the mass of wood behind it, which supports the potentially fragile grain at the leading edge. The same applies to the leading edge of a spoon bowl. Applying the wedge principle in spoon design allows for a combination of strength and elegance.

Thin neck, deep keel

Unlike a metal spoon, wooden spoons have more inherent weaknesses. These are particularly pronounced at the neck of the spoon, where a thin neck must be compensated for with a deep keel to strengthen the neck and ensure longevity.

The wedge principle: a spoon bowl will be inherently strong if there is more material in the middle of the bowl, tapering to its tip.

Having a deep keel means the spoon neck will be strong.

RATIOS: THE RULE OF THREES

The rule of threes is a design principle that offers a guideline on the length of a spoon. One-third bowl to two-thirds handle makes for a well-proportioned eating spoon. Accordingly, a 4cm long spoon bowl will suit a 12cm handle.

Golden ratio callipers by the spoon crank.

CARVING A WOODEN SPOON

Over the forthcoming chapters, 25 steps outline the process of carving a log into a finished spoon. These steps are summarised below and are referred to in fine detail in Chapters 5, 6, 7 and 8. This 25-step process can be applied to carving a range of spoons, from coffee scoops to soup ladles, love spoons to serving spoons. It is the process I use to carve my spoons and the steps I teach to beginners and intermediate spoon carvers.

An axed-out spoon blank.

Unfinished eating spoon.

Top profile of the spoon.

Finished eating spoon.

Split the log into billets and flatten the top profile.

Select and saw the crank.

Axe down to the crank line.

Axe in the bowl crank.

Draw on the spoon template.

Axe carve V into back of bowl.

Carve away material from the back of the handle into back of handle.

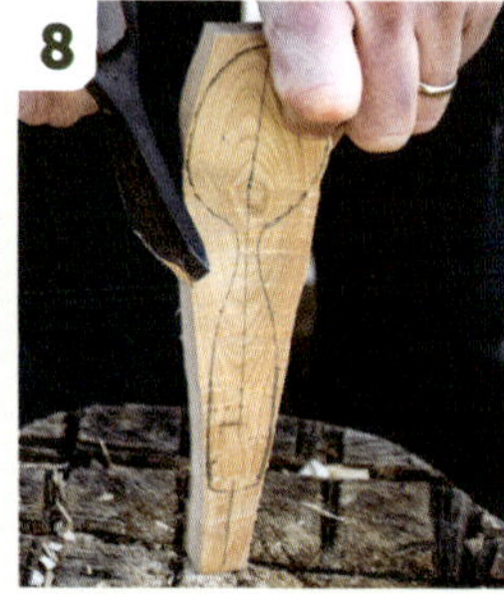

Axe carve sides off spoon blank.

Saw in four stop cuts.

Axe down to bottom saw cut.

Axe off shoulders.

Axe around spoon bowl.

Tidy up the edge of the spoon blank.

Knife carve the side profile.

Knife carve the top of the handle.

Knife carve the back of the bowl.

Hook knife hollowing.

Flatten and even out spoon rim.

Carve away spoon rim.

Hook knife finishing cuts.

Carve in spoon rim.

Back of bowl finishing cuts.

Finishing cuts to keel.

Finishing cuts to top of handle.

Finishing cuts to end of handle.

Stage 1 CHOOSING YOUR LOG

Appropriate wood selection is key to the enjoyment and end result of your spoon. A piece of straight trunk or branch section, 15–20cm in diameter and free of knots, is ideal. A variety of woods suitable for spoon carving are listed in Chapter 1.

BILLET SIZES

A billet is a name for a rectangular shaped piece of wood split from a log. It is the starting point for a spoon carving journey. First, we must identify the size of the spoon we will carve, e.g. a cooking spoon or an eating spoon, as this will inform the proportions of our billet.

The proportions of a 'standard' cooking spoon are around 32cm in length with a 6cm wide bowl. The billet will measure 32cm × 6cm wide × 4.5cm thick.

The proportions of a 'standard' eating spoon are around 15cm in length with a 4.5cm wide bowl.

The billet will measure 15cm × 5cm wide × 4.5cm thick.

A Cherry log 20cm in diameter, 28cm in length, should yield six to eight smaller cooking spoons.

Stage 2 SPLITTING THE BILLET WITH A FROE

1. Place the froe across the centre of the pith; this is normally in the middle of the log.
2. Tilt the edge of the froe on the edge of the log; this enables the froe to 'bite' into the log.
3. Bash the froe with your wooden maul and 'score' a line across the log.
4. Position the froe flush to the log, straight across, and strike it with your maul.
5. Once the froe is a third of the way down the log, you may be able to keep going, or you may require wedges to continue the cleave. Pushing on the handle of the froe will help cleave the wood open (the longer the handle, the more leverage you have!). You have now split your log in half.
6. Choose whether to split a tangential or radial billet (*see* pros and cons of tangential/radial spoons on page 20). Mark the thickness of the billet by scoring a line (*see* 3 above).
7. Bash the froe with your wooden maul and split your billet.

Split the rest of your log into billets if you have time to carve them; if not, keeping the wood in log form will help hold some of the moisture.

Scoring a log with a froe before splitting.

Using wooden wedges to split a log.

Splitting a log with an axe and mallet. Notice the axe handle is pointing away from the legs and feet for safe splitting.

Splitting the billet with an axe

The same approach can be used for splitting logs with an axe and a wooden maul. Employ the scoring technique as above across the width of the log by tapping in the axe so it penetrates 3cm or so across the width of the log. It is easy at this point for the axe to get stuck – take care removing the axe by striking the end of the handle with an open palm until the head releases.

Remove the axe, turn the log on its side to reveal the cleaving crack, and reintroduce the axe further down to split the log open. Splitting wedges may also be needed to split the log open. Carve away any fibres which are holding the log together with an axe – it is surprising how much tension the bark and fibres can hold.

It is imperative that you stand perpendicular to the axe, with the handle pointing to your left- or right-hand side, as the moment the log splits, your axe will swing through at frightening speed, and the femoral arteries in your legs do not want to be in the firing line.

For logs over a certain diameter with straight grain, a splitting maul could be used. The drawback, of course, is that if you fail to split your log accurately first time, the end grain of the wood may be liable to cracking where the maul has made impact and damaged the timber.

Reading the wood

As established in Chapter 1, there are pros and cons to radial and tangential billets. We must 'read the log' to see which choices will be best. When splitting Apple wood, for example, what appears a clean straight piece of trunk wood can have swirly gnarly grain that won't split remotely straight, in which case tangential billets will be preferable. There is also the consideration of the orientation of heartwood and sapwood. How thick is the sapwood? Is the heartwood large enough to feature in the spoon bowl?

It can be pretty to incorporate the beautiful rings of heartwood in the bowl of a spoon. To do so you will need to split a tangential billet, with enough material in it so that the crank can be cut deep enough to incorporate the heartwood underneath the sapwood.

If the log has split well into quarters, radial billets will be a good option. With larger diameter logs there will be the possibility of multiple radial and tangential billets to maximise the number of spoons from the log.

Splitting a crook

Bent branches are the holy grail for the spoon carver. However, they present their own unique challenges when it comes to accurately cleaving them. Cut your bent branch to the correct length of your spoon or ladle leaving around 4cm of excess on the bowl end – this is an insurance policy against the wood splitting and checking.

1 Carve off the bark from the middle of the crook on both sides. Do not skip this step, as it really helps identify and direct the direction of the splitting.

2 Split from the handle end by scoring with a froe or an axe.

3 Wedging the branch between two blocks offers up the wood to enable the froe to make a powerful vertical strike, starting the split down the timber. The split can start to 'run out' in either direction; if this happens you must stop and intervene, guiding the split back on course with an axe or wedges.

4 Turn the branch around, and start splitting from the bowl end of the branch back towards your first split. Although the distance is shorter, the grain in this area can be compressed and tricky to split.

TROUBLESHOOTING AND FAQS

I am not a natural at drawing – how do I draw my own spoon design?

It takes practice to sketch spoon designs. Practise copying spoon templates from this book onto graph paper, and get a feel for drawing curved lines. Drawing a centre line and drawing half of the spoon is much easier than drawing a complete spoon – you can then mirror it on the other side. Once you are confident drawing within the parameters of graph paper, practise drawing your own desired shape freehand onto a piece of plain paper and gradually refine it. Keeping a sketching journal is a great way to catalogue your spoon designs and observe their evolution.

I struggle to draw symmetrical spoons – how do I achieve this?

Top tips for achieving symmetry involve using a spoon template, or sketching a spoon design onto graph paper and then onto a clear plastic template. Holding up your template or spoon to a mirror, or turning it upside down and back to front, also helps identify areas of asymmetry.

What are the weak points in a spoon?

The points which are most prone to breaking tend to be the edge of the spoon bowl, particularly the tip, but also around the shoulders and potentially the neck if the keel is not deep enough. Over time the wear and tear of cooking or eating will tend to make the bowl edge become furry.

It can be helpful to use metal or wooden wedges to help split the crook in two with a mallet.

Wood fibres can be carved away with an axe or hatchet to ease the splitting of the crook. Take care not to chip your axe on any metal wedges stuck in the crook. I keep an old hatchet for this very purpose.

Persevere until you have split half of the ladle away. The cleaner split you can achieve the better, as you will hopefully be able to use both halves of the branch to make two or more ladles. Large bent branches can yield plenty of spoons – make use of this precious wood!

Axe carve the blanks by squaring up the edges and carving the front planes flat. You can now rejoin Step 20 of the carving process (*see* page97).

AXE CARVING

Every time I have had a problem, I have confronted it with the axe of art.

– YAYOI KUSAMA

Carving with an axe can be a daunting prospect. It is very easy to develop bad habits which take time to un-learn. The majority of bad habits when starting out are underpinned by a fear of working with a razor-sharp axe, a perfectly rational fear, but one that can be mitigated with proper technique and practice. Engaging the body in a stance which says, 'ready for action' and using the axe correctly will ensure that you are both safe and effective with each swing of the axe.

It is also possible to develop a maladapted technique due to carving with an axe that is not sufficiently sharp. If the edge is dull, the carver is forced to compensate by changing the arc of the swing and using more effort to split through wood fibres. In short, a sharp axe is a safe axe; it should be able to slice paper cleanly to carve spoons.

In outdoor education, the working space around a carver is referred to as the 'blood bubble'. The name is designed to show that this is the area bystanders should stay out of to avoid being hurt, when a tool is in use. Keeping others at arm's length or at a distance of 2m helps prevent injuries.

Efficient and safe axe carving uses the ergonomics of the body to make the axe become an extension of the arm. Research has shown that the brain's representation of the body can be extended to include objects that are not originally part of the body. Following the exercises in this chapter will support the adoption of correct technique, and in doing so, using the axe can become second nature.

Until the dawn of modern machinery axes were a staple for carpenters, ship builders and house builders, and were ubiquitous on homesteads and farms, performing everything from felling trees to firewood splitting, hewing beams and shaping posts for construction. The versatility and reliability of axes made them a trusted companion in the pre-industrial era, where manual labour was the primary means of production. Axes have retained their significance in arboriculture and in the resurgence of green wood crafts; they are an extremely empowering tool to use.

POSTURE

For right-handed carvers, stand with your left foot close in to the chopping block with your knee slightly bent. Your left groin should be adjacent to the front left edge of the block but safely out of direct line of the axe to keep those crucial arteries safe. Your left knee should be slightly bent, and your knee cap should align vertically with your toes. Your right leg should be straight and as far back as is comfortable, with your foot pointing at 45 degrees from the block. Left-handed carvers should have their right foot close to the chopping block, with the left leg back.

This posture might feel a little odd and a little too 'athletic' but is serves a number of important functions:

1. It removes the majority of the risk of cutting your femoral artery in your legs; if you swing and miss the block entirely, your axe will swing into mid-air rather than into what's known as the 'triangle of death' – which starts at your navel and includes the front of your legs down to your knees – not a triangle we want to venture into!
2. It enables your head position to shift according to your carving technique, placing the weight onto the front foot so that the eyes are directly above the centre of the block.
3. It engages your vertebrae and back muscles to lengthen and engage from your hips upwards, giving you strength and preventing the plethora of back issues that can arise from slumping over the block.
4. With this posture you can adjust to different heights: you can rock back to the heel of the back foot and forward to the balls of the toes on the front foot, giving a range of movement to access different carving positions.

Axe grips

There are three main axe grips that enable the axe to perform entirely different tasks, from removing lots of wood (stock removal) to fine detail carving (accurate enough to sharpen a pencil!).

An axe is most effective as it 'swings' into the wood fibres, making a slicing cut. In order for the axe to swing into the cut, the axe handle pivots from the index finger to the back of the palm, and to enable this rocking motion, the handle must not be gripped too tightly. It is easier said than done for a first-time carver, but try to relax! The same is true for experienced carvers who haven't carved for a while: it can take a little time to loosen up and get into the swing of it. Using the mechanics of your body effectively to swing the axe will massively reduce the risk of repetitive strain injury common amongst regular spoon carvers.

Posture: place your left foot (if you are right-handed) close in to the chopping block with your knee slightly bent. Your right leg should be straight and as far back as is comfortable, with your foot pointing at 45 degrees from the block. Left-handers: vice versa. Your eyes should be directly over the centre of the block.

The hewing grip: hold the handle at the bottom nearest the palm swell. This enables the full swing of the axe to take large amounts of wood off in large cuts for stock removal.

The carving grip: grip the axe half-way up the handle. The grip can be tweaked slightly: further down the handle gives more power; further up gives tighter control by limiting the arc of the axe.

Choking up: hold the handle as close to the axe head as possible. Grip the handle with all fingers, or wrap two fingers around the head of the axe, guiding it to carve like a knife. This is particularly useful for trimming around the edge of the spoon bowl and making 'guillotine' cuts in preparation for knife carving.

PRACTICE EXERCISES

PRACTISE SWINGING THE AXE

1. Extend all your fingers out straight, as if you were about to karate-chop the chopping block, imagining your pinkie finger is the blade. The elbow should move freely, maximising the arc of swing from our shoulder down to our wrist.
2. Next, practise swinging the axe up and down, landing in the centre block.
3. Then practise carving a tapered stake from a 50cm length of 3cm hard wood, into a point.
4. Practising in front of a mirror or filming oneself is an excellent practice, even for experienced carvers.
5. Finally, practise making a slightly rounded piece of wood flat using the relief cut process.

PRACTISE RELIEF CUTS

1. Tilt the billet at a slight angle to the block.
2. Axe carve in a series of relief cuts into the billet. Relief cuts are made at 2cm intervals across the billet and at least 1cm deep; this breaks up the wood fibres and enables the axe to strike through them and leave a clean finish. Do four or five of these at 1cm intervals.
3. Tilt the billet more upright on the block and carve off the relief cuts in one or two strikes.
4. Repeat until the piece of wood is flat.

Stage 3 SQUARING UP THE BILLET

Top and tail the billet. Saw off the top and bottom of the billet down to your desired lengths (use a template from the book, or choose the dimensions of your spoon) observing both ends for any checks or cracks. This prevents unnecessary carving of excess wood.

Square up the sides of the billet. Grip the axe in the carving grip and use a series of relief cuts to carve the sides perfectly flat. Pay attention to grain direction, and carve the sides straight to your desired width.

Square up the front and back of the billet. Radial blanks should be carved into a rectangle; tangential blanks can remain slightly wedge shaped (there is no need to flatten the back side of the billet – the key is to create a perfectly flat plane on the top side of your billet).

Check planes: Looking at the billet at eye level, identify and remove the high spots and level the plane out. For tangential blanks it is not necessary to completely flatten your edges, as you might lose too much width from your billet; however, you do require the sides of the billet to be flat for at least 3cm.

Squared-up billet. A squared billet sets up the potential for a well-proportioned spoon. Skipping this step, or settling for a less-than-flat billet, can set up a cascade of errors, as spoons are three-dimensional and have many planes to keep in proportion.

Stage 4 CRANK

This technique might seem unintuitive and risky as it creates the sensation that you are carving towards your forearm, however in reality this is a very safe and effective axe carving technique as it would take a concerted effort for your axe to jump over the billet and into your arm!

Check that all surfaces of the blank are perfectly flat and tidy up any inconsistencies – the flatter your blank now, the more symmetrical your spoon will be and the less you will need to correct with the knife.

Use a template or spoon to position the spoon in the billet and choose the location of the bowl and crank. The bowl end should be free of knots or imperfections. If you do not wish to add a 'crank' and simply want to make a flat spoon or spatula, skip to Step 5.

Draw your crank line on the top of the billet and both sides of the billet (this marks your desired crank depth). At this point there is no point in drawing on the spoon outline.

Saw in the crank saw line. A standard eating spoon will have a crank depth of around 2.5cm and larger serving spoons and ladles can have a depth of 4cm or more.

Saw a straight saw line. When sawing, ensure the billet is on a flat surface and that the saw is perpendicular to the billet to prevent sawing a lopsided crank line!

Axing the handle crank. Make a series of relief cuts just above the saw cut and carve to the bottom of the saw line. Take care not to over-strike into the bowl end. To get additional control, tuck your elbow into your torso, and hold the axe higher up the handle to minimise the amount of momentum through each swing.

Adjust your posture: lean your forearm of your non-carving hand flat on the chopping block, clamping your fingers around the handle end of the billet. Extending your back foot further back in your stance enables the axe to be carving towards the side of the axe block.

Carving the bowl crank: with the toe of the axe, carve the top corner of the billet off and work diagonally downwards to the saw cut. Bring the bowl end of the billet over the edge of the chopping block; this enables the axe to swing through the cut and create a perfectly clean slope down to meet the bottom of the crank line.

Stage 5 DRAW ON YOUR SPOON TEMPLATE

Draw on your spoon template or freehand your spoon design with a sharp watercolour pencil or ballpoint pen and flexible rule. It helps to add a centre line for accuracy. If your template has imperfections, or has not been cut out symmetrically, draw half of the spoon on, then flip around – that way your spoon will be symmetrical.

Stage 6 CARVING THE BACK OF THE HANDLE

Axe a V shape into the back of the handle with a hewing grip. This is achieved by carving at an angle of around 45 degrees, starting from our crank line and tapering down to 10mm at the end of the handle edge. Repeat on both sides until there is a 'ridge line' along the centre of the spoon.

Stage 7

CARVING THE BACK OF THE BOWL

Carve the back of the bowl into a V shape, leaving plenty of material in the centre of the bowl, tapering to a 10mm edge at the rim of the bowl. This ensures you have plenty of material to even out the bowl rim.

Carve off ridges from the back of the handle and bowel. The handle width should be around 10mm at its end. Leave enough material to shape handle sweeps later with the knife, remembering, however, that it is much less strenuous to remove material with the axe than with a knife.

Stage 8 AXING THE SPOON PROFILE: CARVING TO THE PENCIL LINE

Carve as close to the pencil line as you can, away from the bowl's shoulders and along the handle. The key is to create 'vertical' sides all around the perimeter of your spoon, as this will enable you to carve a spoon true to your template or intended design. It is all too easy to chop the sides of your bowl clean off! To minimise this risk leave material around the neck of the spoon between the bowl and the handle. (We will introduce two saw cuts in subsequent steps.)

Stage 9 SAW CUTS

Draw and saw in four saw cuts as close to the neck transition as possible, about 1cm apart. Drawing them first helps prevent over-zealously sawing off the neck of your spoon! Ensure you saw along the saw line at 90 degrees. The tendency can be to drop your wrist and create a lopsided cut.

Stage 10 AXING THE SPOON PROFILE: CARVING TO THE PENCIL LINE

Carving down to the two saw cuts requires caution. Choke up on the axe to give more control. Left: the grain is splitting straight down to the saw cut. Right: the grain lines are wavy and there is a danger of splitting into the handle itself.

Use the choking up grip on the axe handle, to carve with the heel of the axe; this gives a great deal of control and accuracy. Make a few gentle strikes on the top of the saw cuts, and wait to see a crack appear between the saw cuts, then gently tap.

Carve away any remaining saw cuts from the handle. Choke up on the axe for added accuracy.

Use a guillotine cut to slice off any remaining fibres and create a clean neck transition.

Stage 11 CARVE AWAY THE SHOULDERS

Carve away the shoulders with cross-grain cuts. Support the spoon on the edge of your block; a V notch or 'step' in your chopping block offers a useful support. Brace the spoon against the block and take your time. Using the heel of the axe will provide control and prevent over-striking.

Stage 12 CARVE AROUND THE BOWL

Carve around the outside of the bowl, taking care to leave a 90-degree edge.

Stage 13 SAW THE END OF THE BOWL OFF

Saw off the end the blank, or carve around the outside of the bowl, lowering the hand gripping the blank gradually downwards towards the block. This opens the angle, and enables the axe to carve around the outside of the bowl efficiently.

Top and side profiles of an axed out spoon blank, ready for hollowing and knife carving.

TROUBLESHOOTING AND FAQS

How many spoons can you get from one log?

It's a bit like asking how long is a piece of string: 'half its length times two' is the smart answer. In the case of a log, split it in half and then measure out the greatest number of tangential or radial billets you can glean from it, bearing in mind any twist in the grain. When there is a twist, tangential billets will be more efficient to carve. As an example, a 30cm log should yield at least six average sized eating spoons.

My axe is bouncing off the wood – what's going wrong?

The chances are the axe is not sharp enough or the angle you are carving at is incorrect. This often starts with incorrect body posture. Self-diagnosing incorrect posture requires an honest 'look in the mirror' (looking in a full-sized mirror would be an excellent idea) but is not entirely necessary. Compare your posture to the image on page 104. Ensure that your axe is coming down vertically and you are holding the billet at the correct angle.

My billet is scruffy and full of uneven wood fibres

As above, a sharp axe will slice through the fibres better and when used correctly will provide a crisp finish. You may need to change the angle. Make sure your axe block is at the correct height, and try to take bolder, intentional swings with the axe. This will enable you to make full use of the swing of your arm and gravity's force to execute decisive cuts.

My axe isn't landing where I want it to!

You can gain greater control and accuracy by tweaking your body posture. Firstly, make sure your eyes are directly above the middle of the carving block; secondly, bring your elbow on your carving arm closer to your torso. This will prevent your elbow wobbling around – it must not be rigid, but what it will do is enable you to make straighter vertical power cuts. For greater control you can also bring your hand higher up the handle. We use an axe 'choked up' (i.e. close to the axe head) for detailed carving. Do not get in the habit of only gripping the axe here, but experiment between holding the axe half-way and a third of the way up the handle.

My arm and fingers ache from holding the axe

This is common if you have not spent long swinging an axe – it will take time to build the muscle memory and muscle strength to become comfortable carving for periods of time. It is also possible that the axe handle may be too large for your hand and the weight of the axe too heavy.

Help – I've got a crack! What can I do?

We need to diagnose the extent of the damage and what has caused it. Cracks in the back rim of the bowl tend to be caused by over strikes when carving down to the saw cuts in the handle. These can sometimes be chased out if they are less than a couple of millimetres deep. However, the crack can extend beyond what is visible to the naked eye, so keep an eye on it as it dries.

I've chopped off the edge of my bowl; can I still get a spoon out of this?

You may well be able to get a nice long-handled tea spoon, or jam spoon. The question is, do you want to, or should this go down as designer kindling?

RE-PROFILING AN AXE

The ability to re-grind or re-profile an axe for the purposes of spoon carving is a liberating and useful skill. It makes budget hatchets a viable and affordable option for starting out, and re-profiling is a fantastic addition to the sharpening skill set.

Here a Prandi Hatchet axe is being modified into a carving axe. This axe and many similarly priced hatchets, which are designed for splitting kindling and basic chopping tasks, can be easily modified into good carving hatchets. They tend to arrive blunt or with a secondary bevel. A bastard cut file can be used to remove the shoulders from the secondary bevel and sharpen the edge before moving onto finer sharpening stones.

A Sjobergs workbench pro is used to clamp the axe in a vice. Alternatively clamps can be employed to the edge of a table or sturdy surface.

Apply marker pen to the back of the shoulders and middle of the bevel. Begin sharpening on the same principles as sharpening an axe with a convex bevel covered in Chapter 3.

Keep sharpening until you reach the cutting edge and a burr starts to form on the edge.

Move onto finer sharpening stones or an axe puck to remove the scratch pattern and create a razor sharp convex bevel. Finally stropping to remove burr and polish the edge.

KNIFE CARVING

Nothing thicker than a knife's blade separates happiness from melancholy.

– VIRGINIA WOOLF

A carving knife is designed to split and slice fibres. The sharper the knife, the more incisive and clean the split and the crisper the finish in the wood. A dedicated carving knife, with an appropriate edge geometry for carving, is essential as it will guide the bevel through the fibres of the wood, making a clean, slicing cut.

A telling yardstick of whether you and your knife are carving as they should, is the analysis of the shavings you produce. Pick them up and have a look. Large, flat and slightly convex chips when removing lots of material from the spoon blank, and long, fine, curly shavings when carving facets are sure signs you are carving efficiently and your tool is adequately sharp.

Carving knives offer us a multitude of different tools in one: a miniature planer, hewing tool and curved blade to name just three! Understanding the anatomy of our knife is essential to getting the most from these versatile tools. The straight edge nearest the handle enables the carver to make straight 'planing' cuts that plane the wood flat. Planing cuts produce flat wood shavings. The belly of the knife is curved and enables the carver to make 'hewing cuts' that remove chunks of wood at a time, these chips are convex in shape and can be chunky. The tip of the knife is curved and, as such, enables the carver to make turning cuts around corners such as at the neck of the spoon. The very tip of the knife can be used for fine detail carving and even kolrosing. Once understood, a multitude of possibilities open with one simple tool, and with this understanding we can employ knife grips and techniques that will suit the various stages of carving.

A wide variety of knife grips can be employed at various stages of carving. Experimenting and learning each technique will enable you to create a diverse skills-set and provide you with plenty of options when carving spoons. It is all too easy to get by with one or two knife carving techniques; pushing your learning edge and learning them all will make for smoother and more efficient carving.

It is also worth experimenting with a wide variety of edge tools, such as draw knives, stock knives and push-knives, as using mechanical leverage in your favour can do wonders for alleviating some of the strain knife carving can put on the hands! Draw knives work by pulling, push-knives by pushing and stock knives by downward slicing – these tools can be particularly helpful for alleviating joint strain. Many carvers use a combination of these three knives to do the majority of the stock removal covered in the previous chapter on axe carving and even finer finishing cuts (*see* Chapter 8).

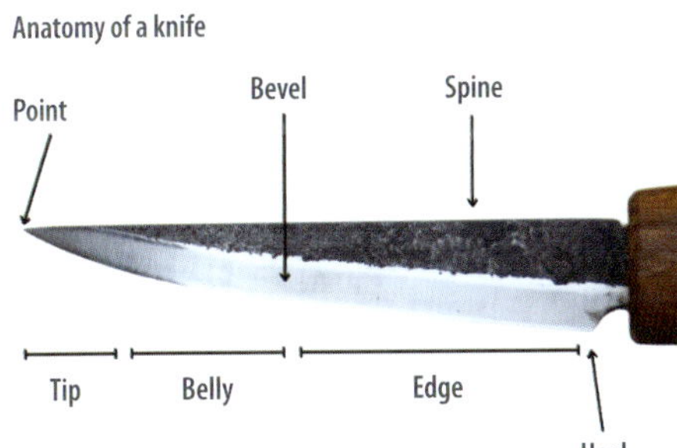

A carving knife offers four tools in one: a straight section for planing cuts (nearest the heel), a curved section for hewing cuts (the belly), a tip for turning cuts (tip) and a point for kolrosing or engraving (point).

KNIFE GRIPS

The forehand grip.

The leg pull cut grip.

The chest lever grip.

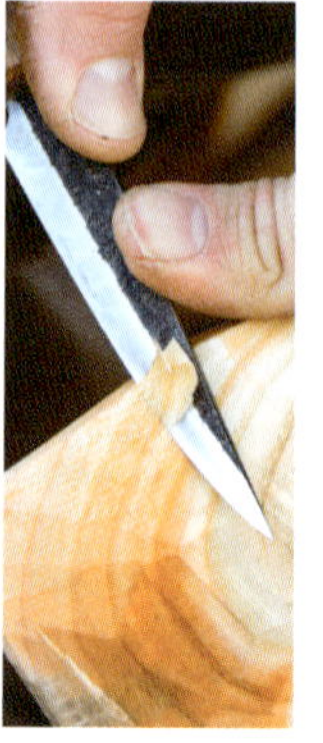
The thumb push cut.

The reinforced pull cut.

The paring cut.

The rocking/stop cut.

Forehand grip

The forehand grip is the most intuitive of knife grips. There can be a tendency to want to point the thumb along the spine of the knife; avoid doing this and instead tuck your thumb up above your fingers.

Usage: General purpose carving
Difficulty rating: 1/5
Power rating: 7/10
Pros: Intuitive and straightforward to master.

Leg pull cut

The leg pull cut is easy to overlook, but for carvers requiring additional strength and power in their cuts, and for production carvers making lots of spoons, the leg pull cut makes valuable use of a natural body lock which when mastered makes carving spoon handles look and feel very easy.

Usage: Long facets on cooking spoons.
Difficulty rating: 3/5
Power rating: 8/10
Pros: A powerful and relatively effortless cut for introducing and removing facets of spoon handle. Great for making round handles quickly.
Cons: Not particularly versatile, easy to overlook.

Chest lever grip

The chest lever grip or 'chicken lever grip' is rather unintuitive to start with, but once mastered, it is one of the most powerful and effective techniques and it is particularly suited to carving the back of the bowl. Hold the knife in a reverse forehand grip with the knife blade pointing away from the body (to the right-hand side for right-handers, to the left for left-handers).

Usage: Back of the bowl, handle and any cuts that require extra power.
Difficulty rating: 4/5
Power rating: 10/10
Pros: Very efficient at removing material from the back of the bowl, but also a versatile technique to draw upon when you need to remove lots of wood in a controlled way.
Cons: Tricky to get the hang of, easy to develop the wrong technique and think it is a waste of time!

The thumb push cut

The thumb push cut is a powerful and controlled cut. Use the thumb of your non-carving hand to guide and push the spine of the knife.

Usage: Back of the spoon bowl, edge profile of the spoon, general-purpose carving.
Difficulty rating: 1/5
Power rating: 8/10
Pros: Very controlled cut, can be used for hewing cuts as well planing cuts and refining cuts.
Cons: The centre of the thumb pad can blister with excessive pushing against the spine of the knife.

Reinforced pull cut

The reinforced pull cut is wonderfully controlled and satisfying. It excels at adding sweeps to spoon handles and around the rim of the bowl. It also enables the knife to work down the grain in areas that other knife cuts simply cannot.

Usage: Around the rim of the bowl, carving sweeps into the handle. (It is the one exception to the 'carve away from the body' rule.) Our body mechanics are such that even if you try and pull the knife towards your torso, the elbow and shoulder joints prevent our arms reaching our chest.
Difficulty rating: 3/5
Power rating: 4/10
Pros: Controlled and very satisfying.
Cons: Takes some practice.

Paring cut

The paring cut is perhaps familiar to those who use it to peel fruit or vegetables. The difference however is wood grain behaves differently to vegetable peelings! There is more resistance and unpredictability – it is imperative that the thumb is hidden behind the wood and that this technique is used sparingly.

Usage: Chamfering the bowl end and tidying up edges.
Difficulty rating: 3/5
Power rating: 7/10
Pros: A strong and accurate technique once mastered.
Cons: High potential for injury if the thumb is not taken care of.

Rocking/stop cut

This is a whittling cut that enables 90-degree angles to be made in the wood. The knife is essentially used like a guillotine. It is critical you do not perform this cut on your leg. Support the spoon on a stable worktop or your chopping block, keeping fingers tucked away, and pivot the knife into the cut, by pushing vertically downwards. With practice this cut can be performed without the use of a block and can be used to make a crisp, angular neck transition.

Usage: Carving 90-degree angles in wood. Particularly useful for making a crisp neck transition.
Difficulty rating: 3/5
Power rating: 6/10
Pros: An accurate and reliable cut.
Cons: As a significant amount of weight can be put downwards into the knife, if the spoon is not braced properly, the knife could slip. Take care.

Stage 14 CARVING AROUND THE PROFILE OF THE SPOON

The axed-out spoon blank is ready for the knife. We must now remove everything which isn't a spoon. Firstly, we'll use a number of different knife cuts in order to achieve completely vertical sides to our spoon blank.

Carve to the pencil line around the entire edge profile of the spoon. The key is to carve the sides of the spoon at 90 degrees to the top profile of the spoon. The flare in the handle and the ovular shape of spoon bowls require carving in different directions.

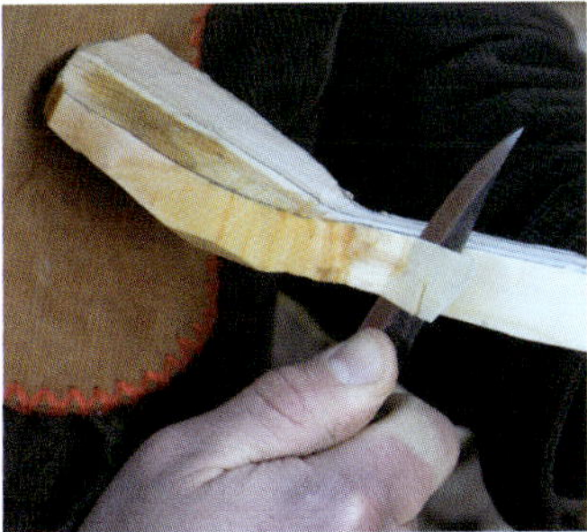

Carve around the entire circumference of the spoon, including the neck transition and handle. A reinforced pull cut can be used to carve towards the bowl, and is particularly good at removing any residual saw lines from the saw cuts, levering up the fibres towards the bowl.

Carve away the loose fibres created by the reinforced pull cut. Holding the spoon bowl, use a thumb push cut to guide the belly and tip of the knife around the neck transition, carving away the loose fibres. This takes practice!

These steps often need repeating until the neck transition is smooth. The neck transition can cause problems, primarily in the form of fibre tennis: it can be frustrating to get stuck in an endless rally, carving back and forth attempting to remove furry bits around the neck of the spoon.

TIP

To avoid creating a 'trench' of furry fibres around the neck of the spoon, ensure the knife is sharp, use the belly and tip of the knife, and start carving 5cm further back down the handle and 2 or 3 cm further back up the bowl. Make as long slicing cuts as you can until the wood fibres have evened out.

Maintain a 90-degree edge to the side of the spoon bowl. The reinforced pull cut and thumb push cut can be used to make precise flat shavings. Carve right to the pencil line.

Carving around the bowl tip. Carving across the bowl rim and tip requires a cross-grain cut – slicing across the grain fibres is harder going than down the grain. The thumb push cut or paring cut can be used to create a crisp leading edge to the bowl.

Stage 15 CARVING THE HANDLE

Handle width is a matter of personal preference. On eating spoons swept handles can give the illusion of being thin whilst maintaining 7 or 8mm of thickness to the centre of the handle, giving both comfort and strength. Too thin and the handle will feel as if it will snap. On cooking spoons an even thickness is perhaps desirable, facets can be satisfying to 'twiddle' in the hand, but sharp edges can be uncomfortable and can either be rounded and refined with a finishing knife or burnished to smoothness.

Holding the bowl, use the chest lever grip to take long planing cuts with the straight section of your knife. Reduce the middle facet down to around 8mm in thickness and retain a keel depth of 10mm. Leave enough wood to carve a convex sweep or facets into the top side of your handle if desired.

Carve the top of the handle with a reinforced pull cut. Handle sweeps and octagonal handles are both efficient ways of creating a comfortable and aesthetically beautiful handle.

Straight bold facets are easy to master and proudly exhibit that the spoon was carved with edge tools – no sandpaper or machinery here! A hexagonal handle is quick and efficient for cooking spoons; five facets on the top handle face are aesthetically pleasing on eating spoons.

Neck transition facets. Certain spoon designs lend themselves well to having a smooth transition from handle to bowl. The reinforced pull cut can be used to blend the handle facets into the neck of the spoon, which can be joined up later to the facets around the rim of the bowl. This creates a fluidity to the spoon design.

Stage 16 BACK OF THE BOWL

The axe marks left from carving the back of the bowl can be tidied up with a thumb push cut. At this stage, before the bowl is hollowed with the hook knife, establish a slightly cambered back to the bowl, ensuring that a generous rim of 8mm is left all the way around the bowl. Holding the spoon blank out in front of you at eye level enables the identification of any high spots which need to be evened out in the rim and bowl.

POV of the chest lever grip – the most efficient technique for decisively shaping the back of the bowl. Retain 10mm at the deepest point of the bowl and use the chest lever grip to camber the bowl, leaving a 5mm rim all the way around.

The thumb push can be used in a rotating motion, to carve arcing cuts into the bowl. This is the most efficient way of creating the camber in the back of the bowl

DRAW KNIFE CARVING

A draw knife is a wonderfully intuitive and straightforward tool. The physiology of most folks without physical limitations, is such that although you are 'drawing' a large razor-sharp knife towards your torso, your shoulders and elbows won't let you cut yourself through the middle. Of course it is still possible to cut yourself in other ways, but I have seen draw knives used safely and effectively by 5-year-olds; they are a wonderfully efficient and intuitive tools to use. As many will testify, making shavings with a draw knife can be very addictive.

Usage: Draw-knives are wonderful for shaping long handles on cooking spoons and when used in conjunction with a spoon mule.
Difficulty rating: 1/5
Power rating: 10/10
Pros: Very energy efficient – can use it sitting down!
Cons: Not everyone has a shave horse, spoon mule or useable vice on a workbench. If wielding an axe for long periods of time is not a viable option, or you would like to vary your carving, consider building a shave horse or installing a woodworking vice to a worktop.

Draw knife carving on a folding shave horse.

Carving straight handle facets with a draw knife.

Carving one continuous facet with a draw-knife. If the draw knife gets stuck, the chances are you are carving too far 'uphill' or against the grain. Turn the spoon around and carve the other way, or reverse the draw-knife and carve backwards, removing the uneven section.

The draw knife can be used to efficiently create cross-grain cuts, as the mechanical advantage of using a 'draw' motion is much more powerful than a carving knife. Here a draw knife is used to create a wide chamfer on the leading edge of the spoon bowl.

The spoon is clamped in a raised Sjöbergs Pro workbench. The entire spoon can be carved this way – working at mid-torso height provides excellent leverage for carving the back of the spoon bowl.

STOCK KNIFE CARVING

A stock knife, complete with a versatile bench and jig, can be used for a range of woodworking projects. It is modelled on the concept of the French *paroirs de sabotier* or clog-maker's knife, which features a long slightly curved blade that is slotted into a bench ring and used in a slicing motion to shape wooden clogs.

This stock knife has a shorter blade length than a *paroir*, and has been hollow forged on the back for ease of sharpening. It is specifically designed by green wood worker Sean Hellman for a range of woodworking projects, from sculptural carving to carving spoons, bowls and kuksas. It excels at carving end grain and maximises the use of leverage to minimise repetitive strain on the body

Carving a cooking spoon with a stock knife.

Carving the shoulders from the back of the bowl with a stock knife.

Carving the back of the bowl with a stock knife. The stock knife can take large efficient slices and make light work of larger cooking spoons.

Carving handle facets with the stock knife.

A stock knife is one of the most efficient tools for carving end grain. It slices across wood fibres effortlessly – this method saves the edge of your finishing knives.

MORA PUSH KNIFE

A push knife is similar in application to a draw knife, but differs in that the handles are adjacent to the knife blade and the knife edge tends to be shorter; these two attributes make stock knives wonderfully controlled and a great option for people with limited physical abilities.

A stock knife can be used at standing height and requires much less stooping and bending than axe carving. It is also possible to convert a push knife into a stock knife, by simply attaching a ring into the handle and attaching it to a ring in your carving block.

An Erik Jönsson Mora push knife used with a Sjöbergs Workbench Pro to shape the outside of the spoon bowl.

KIT RECOMMENDATION

A bodger's bib, constructed from a 5mm thick padded material such as leather or upcycled rubber is an extremely practical piece of kit for the spoon carver. It provides a grippy surface to brace the spoon on and protects the sternum from being bruised by the end of the spoon being pressed into the chest. So too an apron made from sturdy material, such as leather or heavy duty canvas, protects clothing from cuts and slices and keeps the carver separate from the endless reams of wood shavings.

TROUBLESHOOTING AND FAQS

I am getting furry grain around the neck of my spoon

This is all too common – the neck transition is the most challenging part of the spoon. Firstly, the sharpness of your knife is critical: if it isn't razor-sharp, it needs to be. Secondly, the wetter and more fibrous the wood, the harder it is to get a crisp finish and the more likely you are going to be having a game of fibre tennis, back and forth. The key is that as you carve, the grain fibres match up; this often means carving further back down the handle to flatten out the side profile. Waiting until the surface dries out a little will help, as the fibres will compact and a crisper finish will be possible.

My spoon looks like it has been nibbled by a mouse

It can be hard to achieve a really crisp finish when the knife has taken lots of little chips, rather than big bold facets. It takes practice to learn to carve authoritatively; the bolder, crisper and larger the cut, the easier it is to achieve a crisp finish. Practise carving big facets, leave them proud, or smooth them out by carving off their edges.

My knife is leaving little marks in the wood

The chances are there is a tiny 'dink' or 'nick' in the blade, which will be visible close up or with magnification. This must be sharpened out, by going back to a coarse sharpening stone of around 300 or 400 grit.

Thumb push cut hurts

The thumb push cut is wonderfully controlled, and it easy to become over-reliant on it. If you are carving with a bushcraft knife, I recommend changing to a dedicated carving knife, as detailed in Chapter 2. Even carving knives with rounded spines will take their toll on your thumb pad. Leather or rubber thumb grips are available and can provide some protection in this department.

HOLLOWING

You must never be fearful about what you are doing when it's right.

– ROSA PARKS

Hollowing wood involves some additional principles to working with wood grain and with straight-edged tools. Curved tools have curved bevels, which make convex or hollowing cuts in the wood. Once the edge of a curve gouge or hook knife slices into the wood, the depth of the cut is determined by the angle it goes in, the sweep or curvature of the edge, the geometry of the bevel and the amount of force exerted behind the tool.

This may sound obvious but understanding how to work these factors in your favour can save an enormous amount of effort: right tool for the right job, right technique for the right tool and so on. One immediate difference between splitting 'down the grain,' and hollowing down and through the grain of the wood is that the tool meets more resistance; it could be said that wood is more reluctant to being hollowed than being split.

This is due to the fact that curved tools must cut down and through layers of growth rings. It is essential therefore that the tool is sharp and has an appropriate bevel. Trying to make do with a dull or inappropriate tool will prove unsatisfactory and potentially dangerous. There are no substitutes for adzes, hook knives and curved gouges that have been designed specifically with the spoon carver or green wood worker in mind and have been forged, heat treated and sharpened with the correct edge geometry.

Having the correct bevel angle is key to efficient hollowing, as once the edge penetrates the wood fibres, the bevel guides the tool through the cut, a curved bevel creating a curved or convex cut. The first cuts meet the most resistance as the bevel as to work hard to slice through the wood, but once a channel has been formed, the curved bevel can slice efficiently.

The importance of working wood 'green' becomes apparent when hollowing, as with greener wood the tool meets less resistance. As the spoon blank dries, the outer fibres of the wood can form a film and harden quickly, so I opt for an adze to start the hollowing process. The ratio of effort to wood removed is very efficient and the adze, like the axe, can be used for taking large chunks of material, and in a refined and accurate manner.

There are a variety of tools and vices for hollowing out the spoon bowl, from workbench vices to spoon mules, adzes, gouges and twca cams. The hook knife is a very versatile tool, and if there is one tool and one tool only to do the hollowing it is a high-quality hook knife with a razor-sharp edge.

The hook knife is perhaps the least intuitive and most dangerous of spoon carving tools to begin carving with. It is the hand holding the spoon blank that is most at risk from being cut – in particular the thumb and the fleshy area of the palm. However, the risk of injury can be mitigated by 'hiding' or tucking away these parts under the spoon blank.

A cut-resistant glove rated 5 with polyurethane coating will provide a basic level of protection; however, only chain-mail would stop the damage a hook knife can do, and so all safety precautions do have their limitations. For beginner spoon carvers, wearing a cut-resistant glove on your non-carving hand is advisable, and at certain spoon carving workshops it is mandatory.

HOOK KNIFE GRIPS

For first time users the shape of the hook knife can lead to the belief that the hook knife behaves like a scoop, when it actually behaves more like a knife that slices rather than scoops.

In Chapter 2 there is a list of different profiles of spoon knife that lend themselves to different hollowing tasks. The 'tighter' or more hooked the knife, the deeper the cuts. These knives are best known as roughing out knives used to remove the majority of material from the spoon bowl. The more open curved hook knives are for finishing the spoon bowl.

Using the correct hook knife grip will engage the bevel at the right angle and enable the carver to put controlled force behind the tool.

The thumb pivot comes very naturally to some carvers – it is inherently a powerful technique, as the thumb can brace against the edge of the bowl and give the knife extra leverage. The caveat is, however, that the knife can slip without proper control. What creates the 'handbrake' is locking the muscles in the hand so that the hook knife stops before it can come into contact with the soft thumb. Hiding the thumb behind the bowl edge will prevent cuts and makes this a powerful and effective hollowing technique.

The reinforced push cut is my preferred technique: the third and fourth fingers of the non-carving hand push against the spine of the knife, and guide the hook knife through the cut. This is the reason why double-sided hook knives are far from ideal for spoon carving, as the natural tendency is to want to push on the sharp double-edged blade!

A level 5 cut-resistant glove provides a basic level of protection.

The thumb pivot.

Reinforced pull cut.

THE FOUR DIRECTIONS OF BOWL CARVING

The four directions of spoon bowl carving: abiding by the four directions is critical for carving with the grain and achieving a glassy smooth bowl finish with the hook knife. In the final photo, a cross-grain cut is made across the lowest point of the bowl, tidying up any loose fibres.

Stage 17 ROUGHING OUT

Place the hook knife at the edge of the bowl. Take small shavings across the bowl. Hold the knife at a fairly shallow angle, as small slicing cuts must be made at first. Cross-grain cuts help break the 'film' that can form on the top of a spoon blank where the wood has dried out.

The hook knife slices most effectively in a sideways and downwards movement, more lateral than downwards. The shape of the bevel is convex, which means once a few convex cuts have been established the hook knife begins to follow the shape of its bevel and slice as it was intended to.

TIP

Whilst hollowing out the bowl, start right from the very edge; there is no need to carefully establish a rim to the bowl at this point. It is much quicker to establish the rim in the subsequent steps with the straight knife. Work across the bowl as far as possible, attempting to avoid creating a ridge in the centre of the bowl.

Stage 18 EVENING OUT THE RIM

The straight knife can be used to establish an even rim and accentuate the crank in the bowl. Hold the spoon at eye level and look at the spoon front on, checking its symmetry; are the sides of the bowl even, or is one sloping more steeply than the other? Turn the spoon through 360 degrees.

Use a reinforced pull cut to level out the rim of the spoon. Brace the spoon against the chest with the index finger and middle finger pushing the handle of the spoon into the sternum. The spoon can be held flat or as far over as 90 degrees to your chest.

Through repetitive cuts, it is possible to accentuate the crank in the rim of the bowl. This is why it is essential that we have left at least 5mm of thickness in our side profile; it allows us to even out symmetrical imbalances and deepen the crank in the bowl with the knife.

Use the straight knife to create a rim around the entire bowl, flattening out any inconsistencies from axe carving. A thumb push cut is effective at making cross-grain cuts across the tip of the bowl and bowl edge.

TIP

The reinforced pull cut is the exception to the rule of 'never carve towards yourself' – the reason being that the mechanics of the shoulder, elbow and torso prevent us from cutting ourselves. Even if you try and pull your forearm towards yourself, you cannot cut your torso if your knife is positioned correctly.

BOWL GRADIENT

The inner gradient of the bowl is a crucial aspect of spoon design. For eating spoons, how the spoon feels in the mouth is an intimately important factor. Too deep, and the lips will catch on the rim of the bowl; too shallow and the spoon will not hold enough. Looking at a metal spoon can assist in visualising bowl gradient. The deepest part of the bowl tends to be between two-thirds to three-quarters of the way towards the back of the bowl.

As we saw earlier, the wedge principle teaches us that wood can be tapered to a thin edge, which will be inherently strong if it is supported by a mass of wood behind it. A wooden doorstop is a good example. The wood at the edge is extremely thin, and yet with a mass of wood behind it, it will hold heavy doors and take years of use. The same applies to the rims of spoon bowls. A gentle taper will ensure the spoon rim will withstand the hardest use, being subjected to the rigours of drying and wetting, and scraping against hard bowls.

DEPTH CHECKING

Placing the thumb in the bowl and pinching the index finger on the back of the bowl gives a good indication of bowl thickness. Holding the spoon up to the light or putting the spoon in your mouth are good gauges. How does it feel? Do the lips catch on the rim? Does it feel too chunky?

The gradient of the inside of the bowl is important, particularly on eating spoons, as it must feel smooth in the lips and inside the mouth.

The callipers grip the spoon at its lowest point, and although this eating spoon doesn't appear to have a particularly deep bowl, its deepest point is 6mm from the rim. This allows for a good mouthful of food without the rim catching on the lips.

The thumb and forefinger thickness test.

Light is visible through the bowl in this Cherry sapwood stirring spoon. This spoon has now dried and will likely be too thin to stand up to the rigours of cooking or stirring.

Stage 19 CONTINUE HOLLOWING

Once the rims have been evened out, continue hollowing the spoon bowl. Carve all the way out to the edge of the bowl, removing all of the rim. (As we will see in the next chapter, the rim is the very last cut in the spoon bowl.)

Clear out any remaining unevenness from the deepest point in the bowl with cross-grain cuts. In practice, you may need to repeat the hollowing and the introducing of a rim with a straight knife more than once, to ensure a symmetrical bowl rim and a satisfactory gradient within the spoon bowl.

HOLLOWING WITH AN ADZE

The adze is a fantastically efficient tool for hollowing. With practice, and with the correct size, it can be used to rough out the majority of material from a spoon bowl, before moving onto a roughing out knife. In many ways an adze is most suited to the initial stages of roughing out as it breaks the wood fibres up efficiently, which then enables the bevel of the hook knife to progress through the last stages of roughing out.

The adze is held in an assertive and yet loose fashion, allowing the handle to arc in the palm of the hand. A well-designed adze has the correct handle geometry, which will swing the adze in an arc back towards the carver, engaging the bevel down and across the top profile of the spoon. This would be a scooping motion but effectively the adze 'bites' until it has an exit point.

Carving back towards the hand holding the spoon bowl takes some getting used to, and a cut-resistant glove may be required.

Swing the adze and make a series of relief cuts in the middle of the bowl.

The relief cuts can be 'levered up' before turning the handle and carving at 90 degrees to your first cuts. This will release the relief cuts and start creating a hollow.

Continue by radiating outwards, making the circular hollow larger. Take care when carving near the rim of the bowl to avoid split out.

Continue carving with the majority of stock removal from the centre of the bowl.

Turn the bowl through 90 degrees and carve back towards the bowl's edge. Working back and forth like this will allow the adze to hollow out the bowl efficiently.

Take care when hollowing the centre of the bowl to depth check and ensure you have not taken too much material.

Slow the rhythm of your carving and work out towards the rim, taking smaller, more precise swings. The key is to avoid over-striking and splitting out wood from the rim.

Continue hollowing as far as feels comfortable; in practice it is possible to carve almost the entirety of the spoon bowl with the adze, before moving onto a finishing hook knife for final finishing cuts.

HOLLOWING WITH A TWCA CAM

A twca cam is a specialist spoon carver's tool (Welsh, literally meaning a 'bent knife'). It has a constant radius running around the cutting edge for the effective roughing out of spoons. The radius is such that it is possible to use a twca cam to rough out smaller spoons through to large ladles and kuksas.

Hollowing with a twca cam. This twca cam has a 50cm handle, giving it generous 'torque'.

Engage the blade on the edge of the spoon bowl and make cross-grain cuts. The non-carving hand pushes and guides the blade through the cut, whilst the hand holding the handle rotates from the wrist creating powerful 'torque'.

This radial cooking spoon has grain lines running straight through the bowl from end to end. The twca cam can be used very effectively carving down the grain.

The spoon is gripped in a Sjöbergs workbench, in a solid wooden vice. Twca cam hollowing is fast, efficient and low-stress, as the long handle relieves much of the strain from carving with a hook knife.

HOLLOWING WITH GOUGES

It is possible to use a straight gouge or fishtail gouge for initial hollowing out cuts. However, a straight gouge will be limited to roughing out as its straight blade will prevent convex cuts. Bent gouges and spoon gouges are much more effective. Chapter 2 provides a range of bent gouge options, selecting the correct size and sweep for the size of your spoon is preferable.

Gouges can be used with a workbench vice such as the Sjöbergs Workstation Pro. It is essential that the spoon blank is firmly secure; it can be padded with a scrap piece of leather or foam material. As a temporary measure, it is also possible to secure your spoon with a ratchet strap to a chopping block.

Place the gouge on the edge of the spoon bowl and work with the grain by carving in channels which are the width of the gouge. Using a wooden mallet in combination with a bent gouge requires less effort than pushing the back of the handle.

Working with the gouge by hand offers the controlled ability to make 'sweeping gouge cuts', which effectively scoop out wood at the desired gradient. Remove the high spots from the channels as you go.

DRYING YOUR SPOON

At this point the spoon can be left to dry out in a dry place indoors, away from any heat sources, direct sunlight and temperature fluctuations. Two or three days will typically suffice; for an acid test, the spoon can be placed on a weighing scale, noting its weight twice a day until its weight levels out and its moisture content is level with surrounding conditions.

TROUBLESHOOTING AND FAQS

Reasons for cracking

Many people wonder if their spoons will crack when they dry. The answer is very seldom. But remember wood is hygroscopic: it dries at different rates and different planes of the spoon are liable to drying at different speeds, potentially causing shrinkage and warping.

It can be frustrating to carve a lovely Apple spoon and then discover the bowl has warped and it is entirely wonky.

The reasons for cracking and warping are as follows:

- Exposure to heat and direct sunlight while wet.
- Bark inclusions, knots, presence of pith and fluctuations in grain.
- Uneven thickness in the bowl.
- Orientation within the billet – the misalignment of growth rings in the bowl of the spoon can cause the spoon to dry at different rates.

To slow the drying process, so you have more time to carve the spoon green, place the blank in a plastic bag, or airtight bag with a few handfuls of the wood chip you created carving the spoon.

A crack in the bowl caused by overstriking with the axe.

Bowl too deep

It can be easy to over-hollow a spoon bowl; go too deep and you'll have made an olive strainer. A good indication is the thumb thickness test. To create a comfortable spoon bowl it can be helpful to visualise carving out a slice of one third of an egg. The round bottom of a standard chicken egg should balance in the bowl of an eating spoon. Much like in an egg and spoon race, a good eating spoon will only just hold an egg in its deepest part.

The angle at which the hook knife is cutting is of paramount importance to achieving good bowl gradient, this is dictated by the position of your wrist, try locking your wrist and push it sideways through the cut. Many people rotate their wrists too much, which generates a scooping motion rather than the desired slicing motion.

Hook knife not getting deep enough cuts

A number of factors could be at play here, sharpness being key to hollowing. It takes time to develop the muscle strength and muscle memory to make powerful cuts with the hook knife.

As the hook knife is a curved tool, the first cuts across the flat surface of the spoon blank are tricky, not least because the top of the blank can dry out quite quickly and 'film' over.

If you do not have an adze, you can break up the wood fibres with the heel of the axe, making a series of indentations in the centre of the bowl, taking care not to overshoot or exert too much force. Breaking up the fibres looks messy but can aid the hook tool to move through the initial roughing cuts with less exertion required.

Furry grain in bowl

Furry grain in bowl is a common ailment and a variety of treatment options are available.

A razor-sharp hook knife has the ability to leave a glassy finish on soft woods, such as Willow, even when it has a high moisture content. Therefore the chances are your hook knife could be sharper.

The deep point or crank line in the bowl is the trickiest area to get a smooth finish on as it is where the gradient of the bowl forms a gentle 'U' shape and the knife can catch on either uphill slope. I refer to this as the 'trough transition.' This is the exact point where your hook knife stops when carving down the grain from the tip of the bowl, and down the grain from the back of the bowl.

A cross-grain cut across the trough transition can remove furry grain in one cut. Looking closely at a finished wooden spoon, particularly one on which the oil has cured, it is easy to identify where a carver has done exactly this. Making this cut as subtle as possible requires a sharp knife and practice.

It is also possible to carve finishing cuts into the spoon bowl vertically, by carving down from the top of the bowl and back from the handle, without the need for a cross grain cut. To do so a perfect gradient will be required to match up the grain fibres.

Allowing the spoon to dry for a couple of days helps massively reduce furry grain fibres, as the wood dries it becomes less fibrous.

Cracks in the bowl

Cracks in the bowl of the spoon are usually caused by two things: rapid drying and over-strikes from axing.

Cracks around the back of the spoon bowl are often caused by over-striking when axing the saw cuts away. The impact of one tap of the axe into the bowl, however slight, can cause a crack to open up at the back of the bowl rim. Sometimes these cracks can be chased out, however.

To chase a crack out, determine how deep the crack runs into the bowl, and how much rim you are willing to lose. A crack of more than 2 or 3mm might well be too large to remove without drastically altering your spoon design. Remove wood from both sides to create a symmetrical bowl.

Cracks opening up on the backside of the bowl are usually caused by rapid drying. To prevent this, keep the spoon in a plastic bag with the moist wood chips you have made. It is possible to carve some small cracks and checking out of the back of the bowl, particularly where there was a small amount of pith, or small knots or inclusions. These must be carved down to size quickly as the unconventional grain direction is causing the spoon to dry more rapidly.

The less material on the spoon, the less likely it is to crack when drying.

Cracks in a bowl can prove devastating.

FINISHING CUTS

There are two fatal errors that keep great projects from coming to life: 1) Not finishing 2) Not starting.

– BUDDHA GAUTAMA

The final refining cuts are typically made two to three days or more after carving. Of course it is possible to carve a spoon from start to finish, but when carving particularly green wood, it can be challenging to achieve a crisp finish with moisture content still in the wood. The spoon is still supple and the grain fibres are not as compacted and hardened as when the spoon has fully dried out, or – more accurately – reached equilibrium moisture content (EMC).

The process of drying can vary, depending on air temperature, humidity, the species of wood and thickness of the spoon. It is best to let spoons dry out naturally (forcing wood to dry next to a heat source can lead to cracking) as the wood will absorb or expel moisture until the spoon is in equilibrium with its surroundings.

To slow the drying process, spoons can be placed in a plastic bag full of wood shavings, which will slow the drying process though not alleviate it entirely. It is worth airing your spoon to ensure it does not develop mould; certain species, such as Sycamore, are very prone to developing irremovable blue spots!

The reason for leaving a little extra material on the spoon is that wood is undergoing a transformation as it reaches equilibrium moisture content: the loss of water impacts the cell lumens and cell walls and chemical transformations occur within cellulose, hemicellulose and lignin, influencing not only the wood's colour but also its overall properties.

Warping is perhaps of most concern. I have known many a fruit wood spoon to twist quite severely to one side whilst drying, whereas other species can render very little movement and are more 'stable' when drying. Whilst the wood fibres dry, they can spring up, leaving a slightly textured or rough finish. This is particularly noticeable if the tools were not razor-sharp to start with! It is essential then to check the key identifiers of sharpness before finishing the spoon, sharpening and honing where necessary.

Once dry, the process of refining and adding decoration to the spoon is made straightforward. At this stage there should be enough material left on the spoon to shape its ergonomics, design features and achieve a glassy smooth finish with razor-edge tools. I have found it worthwhile keeping a dedicated set of finishing knives for this very purpose.

Stage 20 HOOK KNIFE FINISHING CUTS

The key when finishing a spoon bowl is getting the appropriate bowl gradient and bowl depth for a functional and strong spoon. The wedge principle is key here. Leave most of the material at the apex of the back of the spoon and taper forwards to the leading edge.

As we established in Chapter 4, the leading edge of the spoon bowl is most exposed to the rigours of use, from scraping the bottom of bowls and pans.

Reinforced pull cut down the bowl: place three fingers on the back of the hook knife. Engage the hook knife at the very top of the rim of the bowl. Push and guide the hook knife down the spoon bowl taking thin crisp shavings that 'roll up' like little cinnamon swirls.

SOAKING SPOONS TO RAISE THE GRAIN

One of my best kept secrets for smooth spoon bowls is soaking the spoon before finishing cuts to raise the grain of the wood. Once soaked in water for around 20 minutes the wood fibres in the spoon swell and, once left to dry, remain protruding from the spoon. At this point, a razor-sharp hook knife can cut through them with ease creating a lasting, smooth finish.

Soak the spoon bowl in a jar of water for around twenty minutes or until the spoon bowl is saturated.

Remove the spoon once it has soaked up the water and is visibly saturated. Leave to air dry until it has returned to its original colour but is still slightly damp.

Shallow finishing cuts can be made with a finishing hook knife.

As the wood is still slightly damp, finishing cuts can be made very fine and will produce noticeably different shavings.

To soak cooking spoons or spatulas could be deemed entirely unnecessary. In this case, a Cherry sapwood spatula, which has changed colour whilst drying and gone a little orange, is given a once over with the hook knife to restore its pale beauty.

As spoons dry, the rim can end up warping a little. Leaving enough material on the rim and back of the bowl allows for the rim to be re-carved. A finishing hook knife is used to carve down the rim to the lowest point in the bowl.

The spoon is turned around and a reinforced pull cut is used to carve the trickier quarter of the bowl.

Stage 21 BOWL RIM FINISHING CUTS

The finished rim can be established with a straight knife or finishing knife. Check the rim has not warped and adjust the sides if required. This is where it pays to have left a substantial amount of material around the edge and at the back of the bowl. The rim thickness and angle of the rim is entirely dependent on function and design.

A tiny reinforced pull cut can be made to establish the rim. Angling the knife at 45 degrees to the bowl is very effective for serving spoons; a flatter rim is excellent for shovel-shaped eating spoons. The inside edges on both can be chamfered to give a smooth feeling in the mouth.

The spoon rim can be as fine or as wide as the spoon design dictates. Here a 1mm rim is introduced around an eating spoon. Notice the second finger is hidden behind the shoulders of the spoon bowl.

A reinforced pull cut is used to continue the chamfer around the bowl.

Stage 22 BACK OF THE BOWL

Now that the inside of the bowl is finished, the material at the back of the bowl can be removed. Unlike on many metal spoons, the back of the bowl is not identical to the front of the bowl. As woodcarvers, we must compensate for the structural weaknesses inherent in wood. The edge of the spoon bowl should therefore be a tapered convex wedge, making it inherently strong and elegant.

Leaving a slight leading edge to the tip of the bowl is wise to ensure it is not too fragile and prone to splitting. It is possible to round up or camber the edge to give the illusion of delicacy whilst retaining plenty of material at the tip of the bowl. Thumb thickness and holding up the spoon to the light tests are key in helping prevent turning your spoon into a tea strainer.

Use the chest lever grip to remove more material from the back of the bowl. A thumb push cut can then be used to make the final finishing cuts.

The finishing cuts on the back of the bowl should taper up to the rim whilst leaving enough material behind the rim to retain its strength.

The back of the bowl of a sapwood Cherry spatula that has turned slightly orange whilst drying is given a once over with a finishing knife.

Finishing cuts create different shaped shavings, as the spoon is dry.

Stage 23 THE BACK OF THE HANDLE

It would be easy to neglect the back of the handle, but it just as important as the rest of the planes of a spoon. Simply mirroring the front of the spoon would also overlook the fact that different fingers sit differently on the front and back of the spoon.

Leaving more material in the middle of the spoon and not making the handle too thin are crucial aspects. The neck transition could be a continuous curve or a 90-degree angle. Leaving a deep keel is essential for strength and integrity. The back and side planes of the handle can be shaped and tapered to remove unnecessarily chunky material.

The back of the neck and keel can be carved down to an appropriate thickness with a reinforced pull cut.

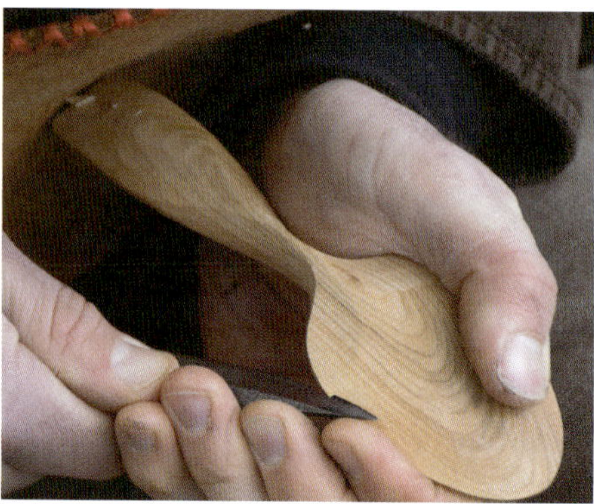

It is possible to blend the handle into the shoulders of the spoon bowl with shoulder sweeps that flow into the neck and back of the handle.

Finishing cuts on the neck transition are made with the tip of the knife, or a thin bevelled turning sloyd knife.

Finishing cuts on a curved neck transition.

A rocking stop cut on an angular neck transition.

This creates a crisp junction between the shoulders and neck of the spoon.

Stage 24 THE FRONT OF THE HANDLE

Carving facets into the handle is both functional and beautiful.

To carve handle sweeps: starting at the end of the handle, tilt the knife at 45 degrees and make a reinforced pull cut down towards the bowl, making thin, long, curly shavings.

Repeat and introduce a second facet row adjacent to the first. Carve the middle facet last. Odd numbers e.g. three, five or seven facets, tend to work well.

Facets can be left 'proud' or can be smoothed by carving off the high tops.

Carving finishing cuts on the long facets of a cooking spoon.

Stage 25 THE END OF THE HANDLE

The end of the spoon handle offers a myriad of creative possibilities, from golden finials to crescent moons, flower blossoms and creatures. See the design section for creative inspiration.

A thumb push cut is used to carve the end of the handle.

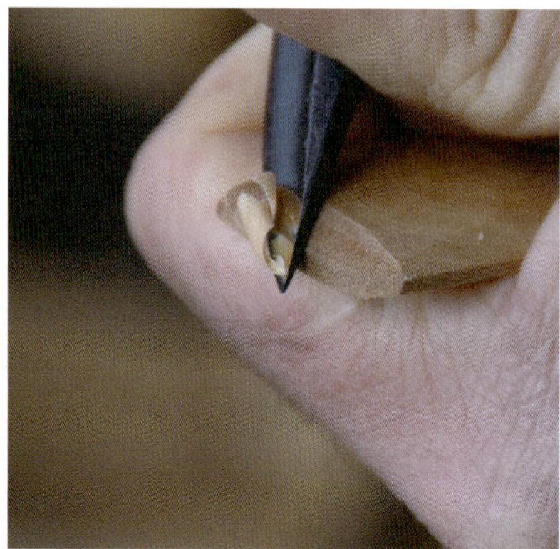

A series of cross-grain cuts can be made to finish the handle end. The handle end could be chamfered or left crisp, according to design.

A spatula is given a cross-shaped chamfer to give the handle a practical design feature, which raises the end of the spoon handle, helping it dry quickly.

TO FINISH OR NOT TO FINISH?

Finishing carving a spoon can be hugely rewarding, but also knowing when to put the spoon down and call it 'done' can turn into a long drawn out ending. It can be tempting to return over the whole surface of the spoon, further refining and refining the finishing cuts.

Following the steps in previous chapters should help mitigate the need to do this. To summarise, we must make sure the following bases have been covered:

- Stick to your template/design.
- Tools should be sharp enough to slice paper.
- Correct tool selection is important.
- Be intentional and bold with your knife cuts.
- Pay attention to the spoon's 3D profiles: depth check/eyeball/symmetry check.
- Carve green as far as you can whilst leaving material 'in the right places.'
- Keep the utility/functionality of the spoon in focus as you carve.

SLOWING THE DRYING PROCESS

As we established in Chapter 1, wood is a hygroscopic material, meaning that it will expand or contract based on how much moisture is in its environment, and as soon as it has been split from a log, the spoon is drying out towards EMC (equilibrium moisture content) with its surroundings.

The drying time of spoons is influenced by various factors including the wood's initial moisture content, the thickness of the blank, environmental conditions, such as temperature and humidity, and the species itself. Hardwoods generally take longer to dry than softwoods, and sapwood takes longer to dry than heartwood. Spoons with both heartwood and sapwood will dry at different rates: the sapwood having more moisture to lose, is slower; the heartwood can dry out remarkably quickly with little moisture left in the cell lumens.

In hot dry climates, the potential for spoons cracking when drying is raised, and efforts need to be made to keep spoon blanks from drying out too quickly, by placing them in the shade, or in a bag with green wood shavings in.

It can be advantageous to slow the drying process down in any climate, as it is often best to carve a spoon all the way to finishing cuts whilst still green, as the ease with which edge tools leave a clean finish is markedly smoother and requires less skill.

SANDING: AN ABRASIVE TOPIC

Although the first recorded instance of the use of sandpaper was in thirteenth-century China, when crushed shells, seeds and sand were bonded to parchment using natural resins, it is safe to say that the use of shark skin and other natural abrasives was not widespread amongst early spoon carvers.

The last century has seen the development of sophisticated and long-lasting abrasives, which have proved revolutionary for many crafts and industries from automobile to lapidary, and for woodworkers and spoon carvers they provide a wonderful solution for keeping a razor edge on our tools.

Left: a sanded Cherry spoon. Right: a knife-carved Lime spoon.

To use sandpaper on spoons, however, risks the wrath of the spoon gods. Sandpaper has been at the centre of a divisive debate for spoon carvers divided into edge-tool-only camps *vs* abrasive addicts.

There are strong arguments for avoiding the use of sandpaper. Firstly, the residue left by sandpaper in the bowl of a spoon is less than desirable. Aluminium oxide and silicon carbide are not meant to be ingested, nor do they look pretty once engrained in the wood.

A close-up of an edge tool finish.

Sandpaper also removes the tool marks or facets left by the carver. One of the most beautiful aspects of hand-carved spoons is the subtle or pronounced facets left by edge tools, which demonstrate the unique relationship between carver and wood. To remove the evidence of this interaction removes some of the soul of the spoon.

It is of course possible to use sandpaper sparingly and cleverly, applying water, raising the grain, removing excess abrasive material and keeping sanding to areas of the spoon which really need it. But it feels like cheating, for a razor-sharp edge tool finish leaves a crisper finish than sandpaper, even super-fine wet and dry will not achieve the same crispness as a razor-sharp edge.

There is a purity to achieving an edge-tool finish, it both enlivens the texture and contour of the spoon and it enables the carver to add unique and subtle details that enhance the visual and tactile qualities of the finished spoon. The truth is that it is possible to hide behind sandpaper as a failsafe way of improving your spoon, but execute a hand-carved spoon with crisp finishing cuts and you will never reach for sandpaper again!

Completed *Cook & Serve Spoons*, ready for oiling or decorating.

Completed *Gratitude Eating Spoon*, ready for oiling or decorating.

Used cooking spoons showing their wear and tear.

TROUBLESHOOTING AND FAQS

Should I let my spoon dry before oiling?

The short answer is yes! Oiling the spoon too early will lock in the moisture and make the spoon prone to moulding or discoloration.

Should I let my spoon dry before baking?

The short answer is yes! It will be at a high risk of cracking if you bake it before it reaches EMC or is in simple terms fully dry.

Is there such thing as too much baking?

Leaving the spoon in the oven for too long, or above 200°C for longer than 10 minutes risks creating a brittle spoon which will crack or chip when dropped or used extensively.

How long will my spoon stay green for me to keep carving?

This massively depends on a variety of factors, including the species, air temperature and humidity, and thickness of the spoon. If you keep it in a plastic bag with wood shavings it will stay carve-able for a week or so; left in dry air it can dry out within a couple of days. I try to carve my spoons from axe carving through to just the steps just before the final finishing cuts.

I still have rough, furry bits around my spoon

At this stage if the spoon has dried out and there are still rough bits the chances are you need to sharpen your tools, and go around the entire spoon 'levelling up' the grain fibres with a super-sharp knife. What often happens is bumps and lumps in the surface of the spoon cause the knife to dig in and create peaks and troughs where the grain fibres are exposed. Attempting to create perfectly flat surfaces in each plane of the spoon are paramount for a crisp finish.

There are tiny scratch marks in the bowl; why is this happening?

The chances are the edge of your blade has a tiny chip out of it that is carving tiny scratch marks in the wood. Return the knife to a medium or coarse sharpening stone (400 grit or less depending on the severity of the chip). Sharpen until you achieve a burr and then work up through the grits.

DECORATIONS AND FINISHES

Through pattern, the world and our own hearts are made beautiful.

– SŌETSU YANAGI

Many carvers have used spoons as a medium to go beyond the confines of practical craft-wares into the world of wood sculpture and art. The parameters of what constitutes a spoon have been blown out of the water by carvers the world over, from First Nations people's ceremonial wares adorned with symbols and figures, to Celtic love spoons with their ornate and personalised motifs.

One of the wonderful things about spoon carving is that within the relative confines of spoon design there is ample opportunity for creativity and design features. Every plane of the spoon presents an opportunity for playing with the functionality, touch and aesthetics which convey the soul of the spoon.

The range of decoration possible on spoons is almost boundless, as are the potential parameters of the spoons themselves – technically a spoon is a spoon if it has a bowl and a handle! Blending figure carving, relief carving and other wood carving techniques is rewarding, and can create extraordinary pieces of sculpture; however, the spoons featured in this book have been deliberately kept simple and functional in form.

Decoration and artistic expression are therefore confined to straight-ish spoon handles and fairly uniform shapes; nonetheless the variation of potential decoration and personalisation to explore is vast, from wood stains, paints and lacquers, baking and burnishing, to chip carving, engraving kolrosing and lettering. Each of these topics are crafts in their own right and have whole books dedicated to them, which are well worth exploring.

This chapter will give an overview of some of the finishes and decorations I enjoy using to give the simple spoon designs in this book unique character and personal touches. I find even working within the tight parameters of functional spoons a freedom of expression and creativity, and this creative freedom gives the finished spoons a soulful character of their own.

It requires good aesthetic judgement whether or not to paint, oil, bake, scorch or burnish, lacquer or ebonise. The beauty of wood grain is such that sometimes a spoon is best left naked or simply oiled.

Certain species of wood lend themselves very well to undergoing these transformations, and experience teaches which combinations of colour and oil, baking and burnishing work best. It is advisable therefore to experiment with off-cuts before applying any finish.

Baking (the process of oven roasting a spoon at 180°C) will transform a greyish Holly spoon into a rich ebony brown, which is a wonderful transformation to observe! Pale woods, such as Maple, Sycamore or Willow, can really come alive with a coat of dark blue linseed oil paint on their handles; tight-grained, slow-grown woods, such as Arbutus or Beech, will chip-carve and kolrose extremely well.

DESIGN FEATURES

Firstly we shall explore the design features which can be incorporated into our spoon design. It is best to plan to include these features in the spoon design stage outlined in Chapter 4. Having plentiful material for adding beads, finials, hearts and other sculptural features tends to lead to a better outcome.

Design details can vary from the subtle, such as chamfers and facets, to bold features, such as finials and cleft surfaces.

1. Chamfered back of handle
A large chamfer.

2. Swept handle
Swept handles are particularly attractive and comfortable on eating spoons. Carving in a handle sweep requires leaving plenty of material on the spoon blank in the axing stage. The sweep of the handle can then be carved in with a reinforced pull cut.

3. Round finials
Round finials can make a decorative addition to a spoon handle. Start with a square and knock off each corner before rounding into a faceted ball.

4. Short handle facets
Handle facets are an efficient way of giving the spoon a distinctive edge tool finish. Use a reinforced pull cut to carve long straight facets from the end of the handle to the neck in one continuous motion.

5. Long handle facets
A hexagonal handle on a cooking spoon is wonderfully quick to carve and is visually striking. Facets can be left proud or can be 'micro chamfered', these make for a nice design feature that can be accented by paint and also makes the handle feel comfortable in the hand.

6. Pinched neck
A pinched neck gives the appearance of delicacy whilst maintaining a functionally strong neck. Facets can flow from the neck transition into the spoon bowl's rim. Ensure you leave a nice deep keel to ensure the neck of the spoon is strong.

7. Diamond finial
Finials can be made in all shapes and sizes, and provide a way of customising the spoon with a little added extra. Experimenting with different shapes can be fun and gives you the opportunity to practise figure carving on a minute scale!

8. Bowl chamfer
Leaving a chamfer at the back of the bowl adds strength to a potential weak spot and lends a certain character to the spoon. Having a chamfer at the back of the bowl means it can also be blended into the handle facets.

9. Cleft handle detail
Leaving a touch of the cleft surface of the spoon can be visually striking and a reminder of the early part of the carving process. Leaving the under bark or bark on the handle can also be an effective and beautiful reminder of the species and character of the tree itself.

Design features: 1. wide end of handle chamfer; 2. swept handle; 3. pair of finials; 4. short handle facets; 5. long handle facets; 6. rim chamfer blended to neck; 7. diamond finial; 8. pinched neck 9. cleft handle detail.

FINIALS

Finials make wonderful embellishments to spoon handles and are an opportunity to give character and a unique signature to the spoon. To carve a round 'ball' finial you must first make a cube on the end of the handle. Allow enough material when carving the spoon for a 7mm × 7mm cube on the end of the handle.

An array of finials.

1 Draw a 7 × 7mm cube on the end of the handle or adjust size accordingly to the dimensions of your spoon. It's easier to reduce the size rather than start again! Make two horizontal saw cuts and then turn the spoon to make two vertical cuts to cut out the cube.

2 Square up the cube with a reinforced pull cut. This is the safest way as your fingers aren't in the firing line when the knife splits quickly through the wood.

3 Carve off the top four corners of the cube with a thumb push cut.

4 Try to keep all four facets the same size and adjust if needed; the more symmetrical the facets, the easier it is to create a sphere.

5 Carve off the bottom four corners of the cube with undercuts. Use a rocking cut to create a stop cut at the base of the cube, and then undercut in with a reinforced pull cut.

6 Carve off the straight edges between the facets using a thumb push cut. The cube will now look like a slightly square faceted ball.

7 Refine the facets into a symmetrical circle. The circle can either be left faceted or smoothed off with tiny chamfers.

HEARTS

Adding a heart shape opens up the possibility of carving love spoons, wedding and anniversary spoons. Like all first-time endeavours, it is worth practising on a thin scrap of wood similar in dimensions to a spoon handle.

A pair of love spoons.

Draw a heart shape on the handle.

Brace the spoon on a piece of flat scrap wood (this helps the drill leave a clean exit hole). Drill out the tip of the heart with a smaller drill bit, and then the two heart chambers with a larger drill bit. The drill bit should be the same size as the round chambers of the heart.

Drill out the remaining centre of the heart with a drill bit. Check that you are drilling straight and that the heart is symmetrical on both the front side and back side.

With a thin finishing knife, carve away the remaining wood and tidy up the straight edges. Use the very tip of the knife to carve around corners, taking care to apply gentle pressure to avoid snapping the tip of the knife. Small round wood files can also be used to smooth the interior effectively if needed.

PATTERN AND DECORATION

Chip carving

Chip carving involves removing small triangular chips of wood from a surface to create intricate geometric patterns, motifs, and designs. Chip carving as an art form is centuries old: it was traditionally used across many cultures to decorate household items and furniture.

Chip carving with the Kirschen chip carving set.

Common motifs include rosettes, diamonds, triangles and interlocking patterns. Traditional chip carving designs are often symmetrical and repetitive, creating a visually appealing and balanced composition.

It is possible to chip carve with an ordinary carving knife, such as a Mora 120 or Mora 106, by taping the blade edge leaving the tip exposed for safe, detailed carving. However, carving on a flat surface with a dedicated chip-carving knife is a worthy place to start and as with all dedicated tools, will offer more control and precision. Practising on a flat board of softwood, then hardwood, and then the spoon itself is recommendable for building technique.

It is possible to chip-carve different types of triangle: the easiest two to start with are an inverted pyramid or a two-sided triangle. An inverted pyramid involves making three identical cuts which meet at a point in the centre, whereas a two-sided triangle's point is skewed towards the apex.

Left: two-sided triangle. Right: inverted pyramid.

Two-sided triangles

Transfer or draw the design onto the wood surface using a light pencil (2H to 9H) or transfer paper and secure the spoon in a vice or with a grippy material. Identify the grain direction in relation to your chips.

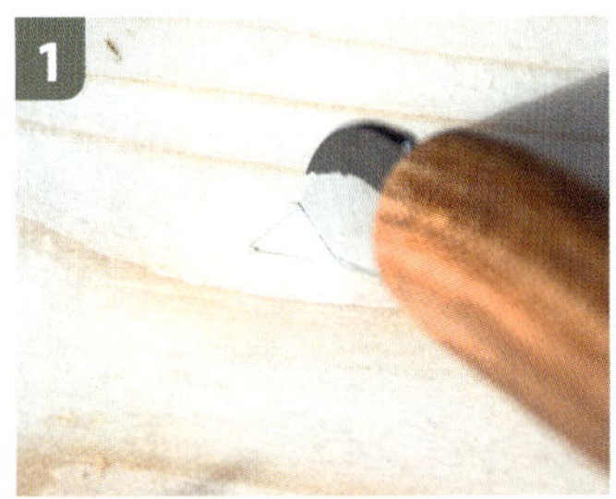

Plunge-cut straight down at a 90-degree angle to the surface for one side of the triangle. A plunge cut 'plunges' the tip of the knife vertically down into the wood whilst the blade of the knife is positioned at a sloping angle. The first cut should be made across the grain lines.

Repeat the plunge cut on the opposite side of the triangle. The depth of the cut will establish the strength of the shadow.

The third 'release cut' should be down the grain line and as such the chip should release and pop out in one incision. Align the cutting edge with the angle formed by the two plunge cuts, then slice through the wood from side to side to form a two-sided triangle.

Two-sided triangle: the deeper the chip the stronger the shadow and bolder the design. Practice and patience are key to mastering chip carving. Start with simpler designs and gradually progress to more complex patterns as you gain confidence and skill; even the most comprehensively geometric patterns are made up of single chips neatly arranged.

Inverted pyramids

Chip-carving an inverted pyramid is similar to carving a two-sided pyramid. Instead of making two plunge cuts at 90 degrees, all three cuts are made at a 65-degree angle, meeting at the centre of the triangle. The third release cut is made along the grain, and triangles pop out satisfyingly.

Make a single cut at 65 degrees.

Make a second cut at 65 degrees.

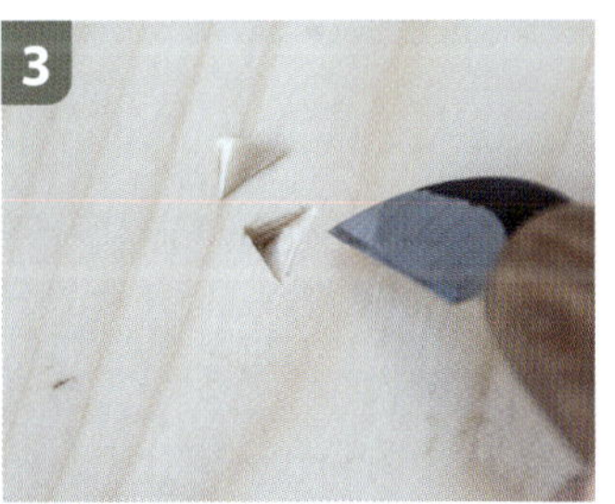

Make the third cut down the grain, at 65 degrees; this is the release cut and with practice, should 'pop' the chip out.

Kirschen chip carving knife with practice board.

ENGRAVING AND PAINT INLAYING

Engraving wood with patterns and inscriptions can be extremely rewarding. The principles of letter carving and chip carving can be combined to create free form inlays with V cuts. Carving a 'V' shaped cut into wood is straightforward down the grain, but requires more practice across the grain.

Employ the same grips and techniques outlined in the letter carving section to make 60-degree V cuts. V cuts can be used for curved lines and straight lines and provide a depth of engraving that will last the test of time. These incisions can be filled with milk paint, sealing wax and metal powdered inlays.

Chip-carved spoons, baked and finished with inlaid milk paint.

Carve an incision at 60 degrees with a pencil grip, cutting approximately 1.5mm deep into the spoon handle. The side of the spoon handle is used a guide rail, by running the third finger along its edge in one straight motion.

Rotate the spoon and complete the V cut by replicating the incision from the opposite side.

The incised cuts can be filled with inlay powders, wax or in this case milk paint. Here the milk paint is mixed to a single cream consistency and applied.

Detail of milk paint filled inlay.

OILS

Linseed oil

Linseed oil is derived from flax seed and is one of the most popular finishes for wood available. Many hardware shop iterations (also known as boiled linseed oil) contain toxic drying agents such naphtha, mineral spirits and dipropylene glycol monomethyl, which is known to cause birth defects and cancer and is therefore to be avoided. These are introduced to quicken the polymerisation (curing and hardening) of the oil on wood.

Fortunately, 100 per cent pure organic linseed oil is widely available and works beautifully. It does take some time to polymerise, meaning the oil won't have hardened and 'dried' fully for a few weeks. If you're in a rush, you can oxidise your oil by blowing bubbles through it, or cure your spoons in a curing kiln; even the residual heat of your oven will speed up the polymerisation process.

Pros: widely available and easy to apply.
Cons: the smell is a matter of personal taste; it also yellows paler woods over time.

Walnut oil

Walnut oil is, unsurprisingly, derived from walnuts – by crushing shelled walnuts to a thick paste, then filtering out the oil from the solids. Walnut oil is the preferred choice for many spoon carvers due to its lovely smell and clear finish. It does not yellow the wood in the same way linseed oil does. The drawback is nut allergies; I never sell spoons with a walnut oil finish for this reason.

Pros: leaves a clear finish whilst popping the grain.
Cons: nut allergies.

Tung oil

Tung oil is obtained by pressing the seed from the nut of the Tung tree (*Vernicia fordii*), which grows predominantly in China. Like many oils, some tung oil producers add toxic drying agents, however 100 per cent pure tung oil is food safe and makes a wonderful finish for woodenware. It has a truly unique love/hate smell which divides the opinions of the woodworking community – try it and you'll know! The benefits of tung oil are that it is clear and it polymerises to a hard, waterproof gel that is highly resistant to acids and mould. It takes time to cure, but this can be speeded up in a kiln.

A sample of oils after curing.

Pros: cures to give a very durable finish.
Cons: nut allergies/the smell can be divisive!

Polymerisation

Polymerisation is a chemical reaction that occurs when oil is applied to wood. When exposed to oxygen in the air, the oil undergoes a process called oxidative polymerisation, transforming from a liquid into a solid film. Oil therefore does not simply 'dry' – it transforms into a solid film. This reaction is initiated by the oxygen molecules breaking the double bonds present in the oil's unsaturated fatty acids, leading to the formation of cross-linked polymer chains. Over time, these chains continue to grow and intertwine, creating a durable and protective coating on the wood surface. This polymerisation process is often referred to as 'curing' or 'drying,' and it results in the formation of a hard and glossy film that enhances the wood's appearance and provides it with protection against moisture, scratches, and other environmental factors. The polymerisation of raw linseed oil on wood is a slow process that can take days or even weeks to complete fully, depending on factors such as temperature, humidity and the thickness of the oil layer.

Beeswax blends

A spoon balm is a wonderfully satisfying concoction to make. Beeswax can be melted down and mixed with oils. A classic combination is 2:1 linseed oil to beeswax ratio, though walnut oil can also be used.

Melt in a large saucepan (I keep a pan dedicated to this task as it is hard to clean hardened wax!) by adding two parts oil to one part beeswax over a low to medium heat. Stir until combined. Pour into a pot and leave to cool.

It is unfortunate that some beeswax is being sold with a '100 per cent pure beeswax' label, when in fact it has been cut with paraffin. This is particularly the case with beeswax beads, which are easy to identify as containing paraffin as they smell like crayons – slightly chemical or plastic. Pure organic beeswax is therefore best obtained direct from beekeepers or organic food shops.

Pros: provides lasting protection/can be used to protect tools from rust.
Cons: messy to make, hard to source 100 per cent pure organic beeswax.

Ebonising

Ebonising is simply a method of staining wood a deep rich black colour – or as close to Ebony as possible. Ebonising makes use of the naturally occurring tannin content in woods. Some woods have higher tannin content than others, and some woods need help in the form of tannin powder to help the stain darken. Ebonising solution can be made easily and is food safe. It requires three simple ingredients: steel wool, vinegar and tannin, together with a jam jar and coffee filter. The process takes around four weeks but, once complete, a jar goes a long way.

Hand-carved eating spoons, burnished and oiled.

Making ebonising solution to stain a Chestnut scoop black.

Dissolve steel wool (the uncoated variety) in a jar of white vinegar. Close the jar with a lid with punctured holes in to allow hydrogen gas to escape and prevent your jar exploding! Leave for one month, stirring occasionally, then strain the solution through a coffee filter to remove any undissolved steel particles.

Add a teaspoon of tannin powder (tannic acid) to 100ml of wire wool vinegar solution. Apply to your spoon with a brush. Reapply to achieve your desired darkness. Once dry, finish with your oil of choice to seal the ebonising solution.

An ebonised Chestnut rice scoop. Chestnut ebonises particularly well due to its high tannin content.

PAINTS

Milk paint

Milk paint has been used for hundreds of years, and is brilliantly suited to painting spoons, as it bonds exceptionally well to wood, and provides a breathable coating which is mould resistant. It is food safe and contains no volatile organic compounds (VOCs) and is typically made from five ingredients: milk protein (casein), clay, chalk, limestone and pigments. The pigments can be natural or synthetic depending on the maker. Milk paint is available in a range of pastel and darker shades and comes in powdered form.

A selection of colour samples of milk paint by The Old Fashioned Milk Paint Co.

Painting a *Two Penny Cooking Spoon* with snow-white milk paint. The neck of the spoon is taped with electrical tape to leave a crisp edge.

Milk paint can be mixed in equal parts paint powder to lukewarm water, or adjusted to your desired finish: a thinner solution provides a colour-wash where the wood grain is still visible, or thicker for a matt finish. I prefer mixing the paint to a double cream consistency.

Mix the powder and water together for at least one minute to ensure the powder is fully dissolved. Then strain through muslin to remove any debris. This really helps get a smooth finish as the strained paint will go on much more smoothly and won't leave any residue on the finished spoon. Milk paint can have quite a coarse texture otherwise.

Once mixed and strained, the paint should be left to rest so that all the air bubbles can pop. Apply with a brush and leave to dry fully before the reapplication of a second coat.

Painting on layers of milk paint

It can be desirable to start with a coat of white undercoat, and apply another colour on top. Once dry the top coat can be rubbed back along any facets and the spoon handles edges with sandpaper. This creates a 'distressed' finish that can look particularly attractive on faceted spoons as the white accents the edge tool finish.

Using medium grit sandpaper is necessary to cut through the top layer of paint and a coarse wire wool can also be used. Focus on rubbing back the high points on the spoon handle, leaving the rest of the paint intact. Once rubbed back, wipe off any paint dust with a slightly damp cloth and oil with linseed oil or your chosen oil.

Linseed oil paint

Linseed oil paint is another wonderful natural paint, made from flax seed which is pressed to make raw linseed oil; then powdered pigments are added for colour, from carbonate of copper to ochre. Linseed oil paint has been used in Scandinavia and Europe for painting the interior and exteriors of wooden houses for centuries. Original coats of paint have even survived hundreds of years.

Linseed oil paint can be bought pre-mixed and often it is advisable to add a mix of pure turpentine to the paint, with a small percentage of methylated spirits. Although it is rare for anyone to chew the handle of an eating spoon, to keep spoons food-safe I avoid using meths and turps, which means the paints take longer to dry and cure and are thicker in their application.

Mixing milk paints to find the perfect green! Mixing two greens with black came close to finding true 'forest green'.

Rubbing back facets with wire wool.

These spoons had one coat of snow white before their final colour coat. The colour coat was then rubbed back along the high points and facets to reveal the snow-white coat underneath.

A selection of linseed oil tester pots by Brouns and Co.

Applying linseed oil paint with a fine brush. The neck of the spoon has been taped with electrical tape to create a crisp neck line. Linseed oil paints can be prone to 'bleed' through, and the good thing about electrical tape is it can be tightened to form a seal around its edge.

Thinning out the paint with a 50:50 mix of turpentine allows for a thinner coat which dries quickly. This way the paint can be used as a stain and the grain of the wood is made visible underneath. It is also possible to thin the paint with additional linseed oil to create a stained effect.

Multiple coats of linseed oil can be layered up to create a rich matt finish which will endure.

Painted, oiled and burnished spoons.

BAKING

Roasting or 'baking' spoons in the oven has a largely aesthetic appeal, with some added benefits to the spoon itself. Roasting is particularly effective with lighter woods, such as Holly, as it can turn a milky white or grey spoon into a rich mahogany brown colour. Spoons carved entirely or largely from sapwood, such as Apple or Hawthorn, can also benefit from light baking with the whitish sapwood turning a golden-brown colour. The aesthetic benefit is that the grain will become more defined as it darkens. This can be particularly effective in tangentially carved spoons.

It can be easy to get carried away and bake all your spoons; however, if there are both heartwood and sapwood colours in the spoon, the contrast between the light sapwood and darker heartwood can be lost by baking.

Another benefit from baking, however, is the ability to speed up the curing or 'polymerisation' of the oil – ideal for that last minute wedding gift or delivery of spoons to your local shop. Roasting can also provide added protection from the blue dots that can form on the tips of handles of cooking spoons left in the drying up rack. Roasting removes the majority of water content and enables a deep penetration and coating of oil, which therefore provides a degree of protection from mould.

Cooking spoons before baking.

Cooking spoons after baking at 180°C for 35 minutes.

Cherry sapwood eating spoons before baking.

Cherry sapwood eating spoons after baking at 180°C for 35 minutes, then 200°C for 5 minutes.

Baking process

The spoon must be completely dry to avoid cracking. To be scientifically certain, place the spoon on weighing scales every day, noting its weight, when the weight stops decreasing, the spoon has acclimatised to room temperature.

Give a very light coat of oil to the spoon. Apply the oil with an oil-moistened rag. This prevents the spoon getting brittle when baking. Too much oil however will bubble and burn in the oven and will create bubbles and staining on the spoon.

Place the spoon in the oven on a grilling rack with a dish underneath to catch any drips of oil. Removing polymerised oil from an oven is no joke! Turn on the oven to 200°C. Heating the spoon up gently will allow the wood to acclimatise gradually.

Once at 200°C, leave the spoon to bake for 20 to 30 minutes, checking the colour regularly to see if the spoon has reached ideal darkness. It is easy to overdo it; some woods will only darken a little, and this will be accentuated with your final coat of oil. Remove from the oven with oven gloves, and place on a dish. Whilst the wood is hot, rub liberally with oil.

Once the oven has cooled to 50°C or so, wipe off any residual oil and return the spoon to cure in the residual heat of the oven. Oil dries by polymerisation and this additional warmth can really speed up this process.

Holly spoon before and after baking. 180°C for 30 minutes then 200°C for 10 minutes.

Burnishing

Burnishing offers numerous benefits that enhance both the aesthetics and functionality of spoons. Burnishing is the process of polishing the entire surface of a spoon to achieve a smooth and glossy finish with a hard object such as a smooth pebble, a piece of antler or the back of a metal spoon.

By compressing the wood fibres with a hard object, the aura of the spoon can really sing. It also makes for a smooth finish, preventing food particles from sticking to the spoon's surface and making the spoon feel smooth in the mouth. It has the advantage over sandpaper, as it won't abrade away the hand-carved character of the spoon.

TROUBLESHOOTING AND FAQS

My spoon has gone yellow with linseed oil

During the oxidisation process, linseed oil can cause the wood to go a yellowish colour. This is particularly true on pale sap-wood. Using pre-oxidised linseed oil can mitigate yellowing to an extent; using other oils, such as walnut oil or tung oil, will prevent it altogether.

After baking, there are bubbles of oil left on the spoon how can I prevent this?

Applying too much oil to the spoon before baking means the oil won't penetrate the wood, and when baked it polymerises on the surface rather than in the cell lumens. It is possible to scrape residual oil off with the back of a knife, wire wool or even burnish patches of oil off. I do not recommend re-carving the spoon after it has been baked as the wood can be brittle.

My spoon has cracked from roasting in the oven

Tight-grained woods can take longer to dry than other woods. There is a chance the spoon had some residual moisture in it, unfortunately, and the rapid heating and evaporation could cause cracking. There is also the possibility that over-striking from axe work, or even knife work, can put splits in the delicate areas of the bowl as baking has a tendency to exacerbate any checking or hidden cracks.

Can I repair cracks in my spoon?

It is possible to repair cracks with natural food-safe glues; however, the likelihood is with repeated washing the cracks will re-appear. The best bet would be to use the spoon for dry goods, or chalk it up as a learning experience and carve another. Green wood can be a harsh teacher but the rewards of carving another spoon will be worth it!

It is good to have an end to journey toward; but it is the journey that matters, in the end.

– URSULA K. LE GUIN

SUPPLIERS AND FURTHER INFORMATION

INDIVIDUAL TOOL MAKERS

Nic Westermann (UK)
https://nicwestermann.co.uk/

James Wood (UK)
https://www.jameswoodblacksmith.co.uk/

Josh Burrell (UK)
https://www.joshuaburrell.co.uk/

Soulwood Creations (UK)
https://soulwoodcreations.com/

Oscar Rush (UK)
https://www.oscarrush.co.uk/

Adam Ashworth (UK)
https://www.ashandiron.co.uk/

Sean Hellman (UK)
https://seanhellman.com/

Hans Karlsson Klensmide AB (Sweden)
https://klensmide.se/

Kay Embretsen (Sweden)
https://kayembretsen.com/

Svante Djärv (Sweden)
https://djarv.se/en/

Julia Kalthoff (Sweden)
https://www.kalthoffaxes.se/

Reid Schwartz (USA)
https://www.reidschwartz.net/

Matt White (USA)
https://www.templemtnwoodcraft.com/

Josh Whitehead (USA)
https://greenhavenforge.com/

TOOL MANUFACTURERS

Hewn and Hone
https://www.hewnandhone.co.uk/

Morakniv
https://morakniv.se/en/

Woodtools
https://wood-tools.co.uk/

Gränsfors Bruk
https://www.gransforsbruk.com/en/

Strong Way Tools
https://strongwaytools.com/

Kirschen Tools
https://kirschen.de/

Pfeil
https://www.pfeiltools.com/

Ashley Iles
https://www.ashleyilestoolstore.co.uk/

RETAILERS

Spooncrank
https://spooncrank.com/

Woodsmith Experience
https://www.woodsmith.co.uk/

Woodland Craft Supplies
https://www.woodlandcraftsupplies.co.uk/

Axminster Tools
https://axminstertools.com/

Workshop Heaven
https://workshopheaven.com/

Wood Tamer
https://www.woodtamer.com.au

SAWS

Bahco Saws
https://www.bahco.com/

Silky Saws
https://silkysaws.com/

Samurai Saws
https://www.samuraisaws.co.uk/

SHARPENING MANUFACTURERS

DMT Diamond Stones
https://www.dmtsharp.com/

Tormek
https://tormek.com/en

Naniwa
https://www.naniwa-abrasive.com/

Veritas
https://www.veritastools.ca/en-ca

SHAVEHORSES, WORKBENCHES AND VICES

Sean Hellman
https://seanhellman.com/

Peter Lanyon Furniture
https://www.peterlanyonfurniture.co.uk/

Sjöbergs
https://sjobergs.se/en/

Michigan Sloyd (Spoon Mule Plans)
https://www.michigansloyd.com/

Green Wood Lab (Origami Shave-horse Plans)
https://gwwlab.com/en/about-us/

SPOON CARVING FESTIVALS

Spoonfest (UK)
https://spoonfest.co.uk/

Spoon Hoolie (UK)
https://www.thegreatscottishspoon-hoolie.co.uk/

Spoontown (UK)
https://spoontown.co.uk/

Lepelfest (Netherlands)
https://www.lepelfeest.nl/

Milan Village Arts School (USA)
https://milanvillageartsschool.org/spoon-gathering/

SPOON CARVING WORKSHOPS

Wood Spirit School (USA)
https://www.woodspiritschool.com/

Green Wood Guild (London, UK)
https://thegreenwoodguild.com/

Alex Finberg (UK)
https://alexfinberg.co.uk/

Gifu Academy of Forest Science and Culture (Japan)
https://www.forest.ac.jp/english/index.html

ASSOCIATIONS

Association of Pole-lathe Turners and Green Woodworkers (AGPTW)
https://www.bodgers.org.uk/

Rise Up and Carve
https://www.riseupandcarve.com/

Spoon Club
https://www.spoonclub.co.uk/

INDEX

First published in 2024 by
The Crowood Press Ltd
Ramsbury, Marlborough
Wiltshire SN8 2HR

enquiries@crowood.com
www.crowood.com

This impression 2025

British Library Cataloguing-in-Publication Data
A catalogue record for this book is available from the British Library.

ISBN 978 0 7198 4461 4

For product safety-related questions, contact:
productsafety@crowood.com

Cover design by Sergey Tsvetkov

Graphic design and typesetting by
Peggy & Co. Design
Printed and bound in India by Parksons Graphics Pvt. Ltd.

Credits

Photography: Jon Howell (front cover), Giles Gostwick
Spoon Templates: Sunny Beach
Mentorship: Sarah James MBE
Spoon Carving Community: Wood species contributions

Acknowledgements

Thank you to everyone who has supported me in the writing of this book – carving spoons together, photography sessions, the hundreds of seen and unseen kindnesses and words of encouragement along the way. There are many more still who deserve special mention.

My beloved wife Bara, whose given so much in the making of this book, your belief in me is like a clear mountain spring and your QC is always on point; thank you from the bottom of my heart. My father Giles for his brilliant photography shots, edits and expertise. Hanka and Vladimir for their generous hosting whilst I typed away. Peter Lanyon for his support in my early days at Devon Green Wood Centre together with the team at MAKE Southwest and the invaluable mentorship from Sarah James MBE.

The international community of spoon carvers who have contributed to this book and who make this craft such a joy, along with the many teachers who have generously shared their carving knowledge at Spoonfest and spoon gatherings. Closest of which are the Lokervya Cornish Carvers who continue to inspire and share in the spirit of carving in community.

Dedication

This book is dedicated to Odette, Lucy, Claire and Martin, and all those gone and not forgotten.